acknowledgements

This book is written and compiled by people who organise events, those who are suppliers to the events industry and other experts in the field. The book is unique in its compilation. It is designed to offer practical help and guidance for organisers by providing advice, information and checklists for organisers.

Sue Stayte and David Watt would particularly like to thank the following for their expert contributions:

2-4 Productions
video production

Automobile Association
signage

AVT Limited
audio visuals and stage set

Boldscan
banners

CCH Editions Limited
VAT on sponsorship and donations

Complete Talent Agency
contracts with agents

Eve Trakway
fencing and barriers

Mike Fulford
catering provision, public consultation

Health Start
fun run checklist

Hire Association of Europe
portable sanitation

ILAM Services Limited
indoor venue checklist

Insurex
insurance

Kalamazoo Security Print Limited
ticketing

Penny Mellor
welfare services

The Mobile and Outside Caterers Association (GB Ltd) (MOCA)
catering

The Made-Up Textiles Association (MUTA)
marquees/tents

National Outdoor Events Association (NOEA)
outdoor venue checklist

Pains Fireworks
firework displays

Performing Arts Management
outdoor concerts checklist

Production Services Association
health and safety, risk assessments and legislation

Regan Cowland Associates
media relations

South Western Management
health and safety and risk assessments

The Leisure Manager
corporate image

West Berkshire Council
licensing

Zap Productions
street entertainment

2

**events:
from start to finish**

Co authors:

Sue Stayte and David C Watt

contributions from other industry experts

ILAM
Institute of Leisure and Amenity Management

Institute of Leisure and Amenity Management

ILAM House, Lower Basildon, Reading, RG8 9NE
Tel No: (01491) 874800 Fax: (01491) 874801
e-mail: info@ilam.co.uk web: www.ilam.co.uk

ISBN 1 873903 74 X

contents

Whatever is worth doing at all, is worth doing well

Lord Chesterfield

introduction

This publication has been produced to enable people working in all aspects of the events industry to have some practical advice and support documentation in an attempt to make their life a little easier.

Being a relatively young industry, the event organisation business has not had time for many people to learn other than by experience. People often come to events through voluntary organisations, public sector involvement and increasingly, through private sector and commercial situations and sometimes with little or no background in the business.

There is a need for some basic guidance for practitioners, both new and more experienced, to call upon. This publication aims to provide such information.

Its aim is to help organisers be aware of the importance of the rules and regulations of event organising and to provide information about where to find detailed information. The text is unashamedly practical and made up of lists, examples and advice drawn from a variety of industry sources and compiled as a result of experience over many years. It supplies a variety of practical tools designed for individuals and groups setting out to organise an event for whatever purpose. The organiser is merely left with the decision as to which of these tools are of particular use to them for any particular event. Very few events – only the most major – will need all the advice given, but it is intended that most situations will be well covered by the contents.

It is also hoped that organisers will draw upon these materials as a reference for training courses they attend, or indeed for training courses they put together internally for a group of involved people – either on a paid or voluntary basis.

A crucial part of the book is the list of other publications and sources of help and advice that can be contacted. No one publication can give all the wisdom required in this vast area.

It should also be emphasised that materials from this book have been drawn together from a variety of sources – groups and individuals working in the industry – to try to ensure that a comprehensive package has been put together. It is hoped that people involved in the business will continue to seek help and advice from each other, as one of the key areas for information must be colleagues practising in the business. The development for partnerships and support networks is going to be an essential part of improving event provision and the ability to learn from others in the field is a key skill.

This book's contents are designed to be of use in a variety of situations to people actually delivering events. The details range from consideration of event objectives to the specific checklists, covering many practical areas in between.

One of the most important documents providing guidelines on event organisation is the *Guide to Health, Safety and Welfare at Pop Concerts and Similar Events* and it is recommended that organisers obtain a copy of this very important publication.

Further information on all aspects of events and their organisation can be obtained from 'Helpful Organisations' listed in Chapter Thirteen.

> The best preparation for good work tomorrow is to do good work today
>
> Elbert Hubbard

chapter one

events

a) what are they?

Defining events is always difficult – they can be many and varied and require a whole range of different skills.

Fundamentally, an event is something out of the ordinary, which has to be specially provided for. It can range from a monthly committee meeting to an international tournament, from a village fete to a major multicultural festival, and from the local dramatic society performance to a high-profile film premier.

The venues, audiences, funding arrangements and the organisational structures and methods can all be radically different in specific instances, but the basic principles of event organisation will remain constant.

No matter how large or small the event, it is vitally important that each one is considered separately and that each event is appropriately considered and efficiently organised.

b) aims and objectives

Every event must have a clearly stated aim, otherwise the event should not happen.

Events demand a lot of concentrated effort and commitment. This commitment can only come out of a genuine belief among all the participants that the aims are worthwhile and that they will be beneficial in the long term.

As well as an overall purpose any specific event must have its own set of objectives.

These must be clear and be set down in a way which will allow us to judge the success of our event after completion.

Objectives must be:
- specific
- measurable
- agreed
- understood
- clear
- achievable
- realistic
- simple
- unambiguous
- timed
- appropriate
- relevant.

In short, it is essential that event objectives should always be:

SMART

Specific	to the particular event and particular aspects of it
Measurable	express the objective in numbers and quantities
Agreed	make sure all team members know the objectives
Realistic	set objectives that the team can realistically achieve
Timed	set a time-scale for achievement of the objectives

c) some event questions

Additionally, to test the practicality of an event a number of basic questions should be asked to ensure 'it all stacks up' before we start.

What event are you going to hold? Why are you going to stage it – what is the overall purpose? Are there detailed event objectives? How are you going to do it? Who is it aimed at? When will the event happen? Where is the best place to hold the event? How much will it cost? Who pays?

Are you sure your planned event is the one most suited to meet these targets? How can we design it more specifically to meet these targets? Have you done any market research? Who are the event customers (remember there are lots of groups, not just one)? What does each group want? Have we thought through all customers needs? Are the staff (including volunteers) trained in customer service?

Have we asked the customers what they want? Are we planning to provide any more than they expect? Have we devised ways of giving them a 'bonus'? Do we examine every possible need and devise ways to meet it? Will we ask at the end for feedback?

d) so what do I do now?

Having answered these questions you should now be much clearer about what you are doing, and how and why you are doing it. You should have quite a clear and positive picture and be ready to proceed confidently.

However, if this is not the case and you are doing the event because somebody has told you to or you are still unclear about some of the answers to these questions, don't despair. It is quite normal for organisers to have some gaps in their ideas when they first sit down to plan an event. Probably the best course of action is to refer to the end of this book and seek some help. Don't be embarrassed about learning from other people's expertise. It is always better than learning from your own mistakes.

Even the best plan degenerates into work

Anon

chapter two
planning

Events are important to the participants, the organisers and the activity so they need a professional and thorough approach in their planning.

Earlier we gave a somewhat simplistic view of events when suggesting they are something that happens out of the ordinary. This is true, but it suggests that they happen by themselves; nothing could be further from the truth. People will be required to make them happen.

Additionally, perhaps the crucial difference between what you might call 'routine' events and 'special' events are that special events must always be planned or they will not end up being 'special'.

This planning will fall into a variety of stages, but it must be stressed that, regardless of the size of event, each of these stages must be gone through. Obviously, depending on the size of the event, the length and depth of each planning stage will vary.

a) event planning stages

- determine aims and objectives
- formulate policy
- carry out a feasibility study
- make decision to go ahead
- compile budget
- identify personnel
- identify resources
- identify event requirements
- identify tasks
- define structure
- communicate structure
- detail plan and time-scale
- establish control systems

- plan event – presentation, preparation, implementation and recovery
- finalise accounts
- hold debriefing
- compile and circulate final evaluation report

REMEMBER

Proper
Planning
Promotes
Perfect
Performance

Or

Proper
Planning
Prevents
Pathetic
Performance

You will have to identify the resources required:
- physical
- professional
- financial

The key task will be the ability to obtain and organise these resources to deliver a successful event.

All events should be F A M O U S

Feasible   it should be possible for the team concerned to achieve the aims

Appropriate   the organisers and participants should be suited to the task

Meaningful   the event should have value to customers (and to team members)

Organised   aims should be well thought-out and clearly stated

United   there should be a shared understanding of the aims, matched by the commitment to achieve them

Supported   adequate resources should be identified

REMEMBER WHEN PLANNING YOUR PROJECT, SUCCESSFUL EVENTS NEED...

- appropriate implementation mechanisms
- budgeting
- business plan/feasibility study
- clear objectives
- committed personnel
- contingency plans
- creativity and innovation
- customer care
- detailed programming
- emergency procedures
- entertainment
- evaluation and control   – formative
                                      – summative
- financial control
- flexibility

- good management and strong leadership
- hard work and enthusiasm
- leadership and co-ordination
- logistical planning
- marketing (especially promotion)
- measurable targets
- media interest
- participants
- planning and documentation
- post-event evaluation
- pricing policy
- public consultation
- quality not quantity
- resources and facilities
- risk assessment
- sense of humour
- structure and good communications
- support (from public, volunteers, politicians, etc)
- teamwork and good inter-personal relationships
- time

b) organisational plan

An event, like any business organisation, needs a clear plan in the background, a clear context in which to deliver and monitor its purpose:

policy
an overall statement of intent
(mission/vision statement)

↓

strategic planning
identification of organised targets

↓

objectives
(specific, measurable, agreed, realistic timeset)
set in consultation with those who have to achieve them

↓

tactical action plans
and allocation of resources

↓

assignment of responsibility and authority
job description (including performance standards)

↓

organisational structure
clarifying roles, responsibilities and lines of communication

↓

control techniques
and performance assessment and measurement

↓

**personal performance   group performance
appraisal   appraisal**

↓

action to improve performance and to develop people
(eg reorganising, training, supporting)

↓

continuing reviews of:
policy, strategic planning objectives, performance

↓

all feedback in for ongoing improvement

c) crisis management

Points to consider when planning for a crisis:
- When planning an event, anticipate the worst possible scenario and act accordingly.
- Devise a detailed crisis management plan and identify responsibilities within it.
- Be prepared to demonstrate human concern for what has happened.
- Whenever possible look for ways of using the media as part of your armoury for containing the effects of the crisis.
- Establish a 'war room' or emergency control centre and staff it with senior personnel trained to fulfil specific roles designed to contain and manage the crisis.
- Know your event and listen to staff on the ground.
- Avoid the use of jargon. Use language that shows you care about what has happened and which clearly demonstrates that you are trying to put matters right.
- Know your audience/customers and their requirements.
- Whenever possible, seek outside expert advice when drawing up crisis contingency plans. Don't reinvent the wheel.
- Training for all staff is an integral part of planning to deal with crisis.

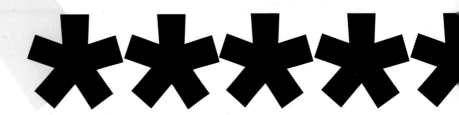

d) event business and budget planning process

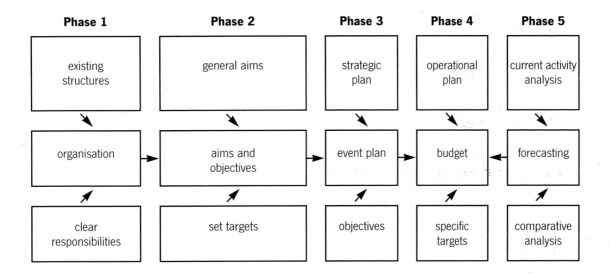

Phase 1	Phase 2	Phase 3	Phase 4	Phase 5
existing structures	general aims	strategic plan	operational plan	current activity analysis
organisation	aims and objectives	event plan	budget	forecasting
clear responsibilities	set targets	objectives	specific targets	comparative analysis

e) event planning timetable

task	year in advance	9 months	6 months	3 months	1 month	1 week
compile budget						
identify personnel						
book venue						
first team meeting						
etc						

f) event planning chart

Taken from: *Leisure and Tourism for Intermediate GNVQ* by Outhart et al

OUTLINE THE OBJECTIVES

remember SMART and FAMOUS

DESCRIBE THE EVENT

customers; timings; activities; movements

CALCULATE RESOURCES

finance; equipment; time; information; people; materials

IDENTIFY CONSTRAINTS

staff; opening times; facility capacity; transport; equipment; health, safety and security

CONTINGENCY ACTIONS

emergencies; disruptions; changes

ALLOCATE ROLES

function; team structures; communication/reporting

g) event planning requirements

Having identified the overall planning progressions, it is necessary to be more specific and identify the precise process by detailing all the requirements for the event. This can be a time-consuming procedure, but should involve a number of people who can think in the widest possible way in an attempt to try and identify all the possible items which will be required to deliver a successful event.

Such a list, which can never really be all encompassing, is necessary to allow detailed planning and implementation to go ahead (see the master list later in the book). The aim here is to identify every single heading that needs to be covered and under each heading, every single item that will be required to produce an efficient, effective event of a quality appropriate to the level of the event.

This means going through a very precise thought process, no matter how large or small, endeavouring to ensure that nothing is omitted which may be required.

h) event organiser's checklist

- ☐ specify the nature of the event
- ☐ define event objectives
- ☐ select a delivery strategy
- ☐ develop a list of specific requirements
- ☐ work out a schedule
- ☐ produce a detailed budget
- ☐ identify the event team
- ☐ decide on roles and responsibilities
- ☐ devise organisational structure
- ☐ specify operational plan
- ☐ write operations manual
- ☐ train team members
- ☐ deliver outcomes
- ☐ monitor progress
- ☐ take corrective action
- ☐ provide feedback
- ☐ dispose of surplus equipment, materials and supplies
- ☐ evaluate event performance
- ☐ carry out event debrief
- ☐ complete final audit
- ☐ complete event report

i) cost and time sheet

event stage	cost				schedule	
	budget	actual	variance	total	planned	actual

j) Gantt Charts

A Gantt Chart is a horizontal bar chart which graphically displays the time relationship of the stages in an event. It is named after Henry Gantt, the industrial engineer who introduced the chart in the early 1900s. Each stage of the event is represented by a line placed on the chart in the time period when it is to be undertaken. Once complete, the Gantt chart shows the flow of activities in sequence as well as those that can be under way at the same time.

To create a Gantt chart, list the stages required to achieve an event and estimate the time required for each. Then list the stages down the left side of the chart and time intervals along the bottom. Draw a line across the chart for each stage, starting at the planned beginning date and ending on the completion date.

Some parallel steps can be carried out at the same time with one taking longer than the other. This allows some flexibility about when to start the shorter stage as long as the plan has it finished in time to flow into subsequent stages. This situation can be shown with a dotted line continuing onto the line when the step must be completed.

When your Gantt chart is finished, you will be able to see the minimum total time for the project, the proper sequence of stages and which stages can be under way at the same time.

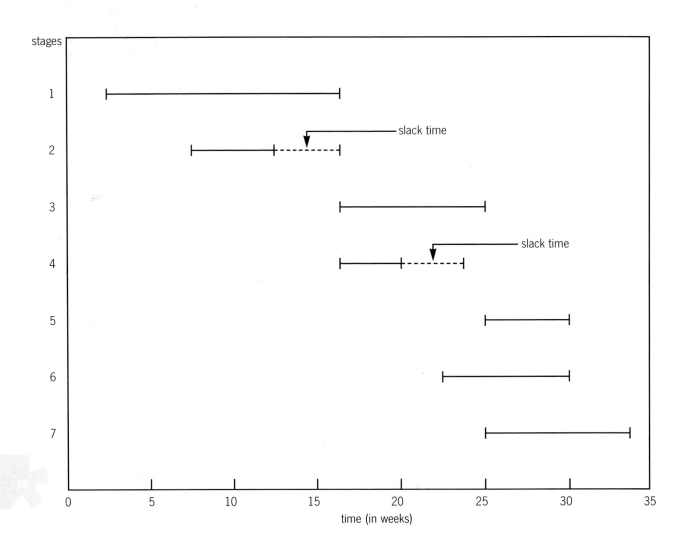

> He has a head to contrive, a tongue to persuade, and a hand to execute any mischief
>
> Edward Hyde,
> Earl of Clarendon

chapter three

personal management

People involved in events will require a number of personal management skills.

These personal management skills will be required at a variety of levels depending on the degree of involvement that the individual has and the scale of the event. However, no matter what the individual's involvement in events, improved personal management skills will help increase the effectiveness of their input.

In essence, personal management leads to increased personal effectiveness, which in turn leads to increased organisation effectiveness and event delivery.

It is absolutely essential that individuals can organise themselves and prioritise their workload to lead to maximum efficiency in their own personal organisation: it seems unlikely that anyone who cannot organise themselves will be able to organise an event.

a) time management

Time management is a key area of personal management which is often not practised well, even by people who can manage quite effectively in other ways. Busy people, as events organisers tend to be, always want more time in the day and since there are only a finite number of hours, minutes and seconds in any one day the only way to find them is to get the maximum use out of each minute that passes.

Time management can involve some fairly complicated procedures and this book is not the place to consider them all. However, there are some principles worth mentioning.

- It is always beneficial to start by analysing your normal time use to see if there are any aspects of your

programme which can be altered particularly if there are any time-wasters in terms of structures, systems or people, that can be minimised within your personal operation.
- An overabundance of paper is a very common example of something that could be dramatically reduced to give someone more time for constructive work.
- It is helpful to organise all telephone calls, and indeed any tasks to be undertaken, by grading them one to five, and doing the ones which are the most important first of all.
- It is also common for many people to just achieve the easy tasks and leave the more difficult ones on the back burner all the time. Achieving the big tasks does create more time and also makes the individual feel-good factor rise.

b) meetings

In so many event settings there seems to be so much time spent (often wasted) in meetings. If we are going to plan an event then meetings will be necessary, but certain simple principles will remove excessive meetings and ensure that those we must have are held efficiently and effectively.

In terms of managing meetings we have to:
- minimise the number of meetings
- ensure those that we do have are as short as possible
- have an agenda, a time limit for the overall meeting and a time limit for each agenda item
- each individual should prepare for each meeting
- have your own individual objectives as well as those for the overall meeting
- every meeting should have minutes or notes taken
- a timed action plan should result from each meeting – if this is not the case then why did everyone attend in the first place?

example of meeting record sheet

date:	present	start:	finish:	apologies	
	decision/conclusion			action	

c) leadership

If you are going to manage, organise or lead an event you will have to portray some significant leadership skills.

positive qualities:	negative qualities:
organised	self-centred
always gets results	moody
patient	gossip
approachable	dictatorial
decisive	intimidatory
interested	doesn't understand
enthusiastic	condescending
assertive	poor attention to detail
communicative	uncommunicative
listens and acts	shy and nervous
firm but fair	fixed views
punctual	unappreciative
confident	
good motivator	

d) the team

You might want your team members to have the following qualities, skills, abilities and characteristics:

enthusiastic	flexible	available
courteous	responsible	good communicator
sense of humour	organised	personable
willing	energetic	initiative
reliable	trustworthy	dependable
unflappable	friendly	teamworker
honest	punctual	efficient
personable	knowledgeable	committed
interested	pro-active	articulate
diligence	resourceful	

ability to cope under pressure

As a leader, you will be responsible for people's performance. Utilise the following management actions as necessary to your specific event to ensure you get the best from your team, whether they are paid or volunteers:

consult	inform	appraise
inspire	lead	listen
control	delegate	recruit
make decisions	understand	guide
co-ordinate	monitor	liaise
care	communicate	encourage
evaluate	schedule	supervise
direct	anticipate	discuss
analyse	brainstorm	question
solve problems	review	set goals

> Money is like a sixth sense without which you cannot make a complete use of the other five
>
> W. Somerset Maughan

chapter four

financial planning

a) the budget

Events should be treated like any other business venture. They should have a business plan and in particular they must have clear, precise and accurate budgeting.

If expenditure exceeds income at the budget planning stage, you will need to evaluate the event and decide where you can save costs, but do not compromise the quality or the safety of the event. It is always best to be cautious about income estimates and pessimistic about costs.

Lots of large costs can arise. Policing, for example, could be a large drain on your budget. Police charges vary greatly throughout the UK. Some police authorities charge around £90 per constable per day.

Review your budget monthly to start with and, as the event approaches, a weekly monitoring system should be in place. Constantly revise and monitor: don't be caught by unexpected cost trends. Bad budget estimating or controlling spells disaster for all concerned.

Careful budgeting is essential for an event to work and for the event to have any credibility. The process of working out the details will be the true test of whether the event plans will be possible.

It is necessary to budget carefully to find out what the event needs in terms of funding and to provide a monitoring system throughout the organising stages.

The first step in the process of examining funding requirements is to establish exactly what the event will cost to stage. There will be a vast range of expenditure to be anticipated. Basically the process of estimating a budget can be done after all the tasks to be performed have been identified.

Every item must be listed with figures for the likely expenditure and possible income placed opposite in separate columns. This will give an exact statement of the forecast figures. It is essential to identify these figures as exactly as possible; incorrect figures can be misleading and cause severe problems later in achieving the event.

Each activity should be broken down and analysed to determine:
- the exact activity to be carried out
- the estimated cost of each activity
- the benefit from each activity
- the income (if any) from the activity
- the necessity of the activity (if it is expensive by event standards)
- the place of the activity in a budget priority list
- how the expenditure on the activity will be monitored

With this process completed, it should be possible to weigh the costs and benefits of the whole project before making any final decisions.

There are certain fixed costs which will have to be met to stage almost any event, eg venue hire, staffing, promotion, insurance, etc. As soon as it is agreed to go ahead these costs will have to be incurred, whatever income can be raised to set against them.

There will be other costs which will not remain constant – variable costs. These will vary according to the size and nature of the event and it may be that they will have to be adapted during the work on the project. Variable costs are exemplified by things like catering, entertainment and accommodation.

The most crucial point about budgeting is to be as accurate as possible but always to over-estimate expenditure and under-estimate income: to do the reverse is a recipe for

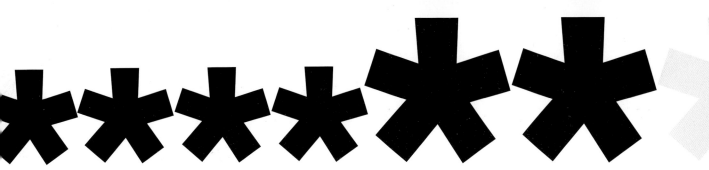

disaster. Pessimistic budgeting is to be recommended, as long as it is not unrealistically gloomy.

The process of budgeting can be achieved as outlined above by identifying the cost and benefit of all items.

b) VAT

Value Added Tax (VAT) and the effect it has on both income and expenditure must be taken into account. For many smaller events VAT registration will not be required, though voluntary registration is permitted. The local Customs and Excise Office will be happy to advise on the necessity to register and on the liability of various items to VAT.

c) inflation

Inflation can have quite profound consequences for budgeting. It can throw estimated figures totally out if, for example, a swing of around ten per cent has occurred within a twelve- to eighteen-month period.

Estimates should be calculated on current figures but an awareness of the possible effects of inflation must be borne in mind. Calculations should be done and attached to the estimates, indicating what may happen to the funding of the event given likely inflationary trends.

d) insurance

Insurance advice is given later in this book (see Chapter 7 – *health & safety*). Public liability, and even perhaps limited personal accident insurance must be arranged, another item all too easily forgotten with potentially very expensive consequences.

e) currency rates

Currency rates can affect the amount of income which comes to some international events, particularly conferences where delegate turnout can be affected by the cost in exchange rates. A poor turnout of delegates obviously puts

the viability of such events in question, as it cuts the income sizably.

f) contingencies

It is essential to put a figure into the budget estimates for additional unforeseen items of cost. Depending on the size of the project in hand, it is advisable to allow between five and ten per cent of the total expenditure as an add-in for contingencies.

g) timetable

A financial timetable for events is necessary. It is necessary to include the time at which expenditure will occur as well as when the money will come in, where the money will come from and what it is paying for. This is an essential part of budgeting for financial feasibility – calculating interest rates on any borrowings or investments; working out when income is required and later controlling expenditure by a pre-set timetable. If a suitable timetable cannot be worked out for such expenditure, then it is virtually certain that the event will not be financially viable. In any venture, cashflow is crucial to viability.

h) funding

For many events, finding the funding is the crucial item and is the one which requires most work; it causes most headaches and worries leading up to any decisions to proceed with an event.

Given the correct event, the correct aim, with the correct objectives, then funding can be found. It must be a package and not just an after-thought. There must be a clear mission and purpose to the whole operation from the start.

There are many agencies that can have a significant interest in supporting events to ensure they happen successfully in a given location. The more obvious ones are local authorities and local tourist boards, but there are others, for example:
• local LECs and TECs
• tourist associations

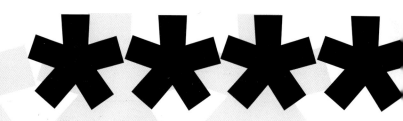

- hoteliers
- local Chambers of Commerce
- national agencies, eg Arts Council, Sports Councils
- major local employers
- Sportsmatch
- Association of Business Sponsorship for the Arts
- National Lottery Distributing Bodies.

Grant-aiding bodies will work within a timeframe whereby grants are approved in advance for any particular financial year, giving the organisers financial certainty that their events will be supported.

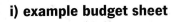

i) example budget sheet

item	budget forecast	revision 1 (date)	revision 2 (date)	revision 3 (date)	revision 4 (date)
income					
ticket sales					
sponsorship					
donations					
grant aid					
secondary spend (catering/merchandising)					
total income					

expenditure					
advertising/promotion publicity/public relations					
signage					
venue hire					
artistes/performers					
portable toilets					
production (staging, lighting, sound, etc)					
seating					
licences					
stewarding					
design and print					
litter collection/recycling					
first aid					
awards/presentations					
barriers/fencing					
catering					
insurance					
gratuities					
Portacabins					
marquees					
travel/subsistence photography					
costs of sponsor (marquees, etc)					
charity donations					
policing					
fireworks/lasers/strobes					

total expenditure					

> Business has only two functions – marketing and innovation
>
> Peter F. Drucker

chapter five

marketing

Marketing must not be seen as a separate entity but as an integral part of staging the event from concept to delivery. It is not just about promotion (an additional section on this later); it is about trying to deliver an event product that the customers want at an affordable price and then making sure they know about it.

These days people are far more sophisticated about the way they spend their disposable income. Young people have far more power than previously, children are persuaded to buy by powerful brand images related through the media. The Spice Girls success has been largely due to a highly skilled marketeer who knew his exact target market and exploited it to the full.

Identifying your target market and supplying its need is the key to successfully selling your product (your event).

When you start to plan your marketing campaign, there are a few points to consider first of all. The event must:
• have a secure financial base
• receive 'political' support
• offer quality service
• provide perceived added value
• identify a clear market niche
• have a realistic infrastructure and timeframe
• be properly organised

a) marketing mix

Effective marketing is about creating a successful marketing mix – getting the right blend of a variety of components – to ensure that an enjoyable and attractive event is delivered for customers.

This blend is about considering carefully each of the following 'Ps' and delivering them appropriately for any specific event. The main Ps are:

Product	the quality event
Place	a suitable venue
Price	considered, set and packaged
Promotion	raising awareness
Programming	fitting into an activity and/or a calendar
Packaging	fitting together with other activities/events/projects
People	the key delivery factor

b) marketing strategy

The preparation of a marketing strategy is essential to any successful event and should take account of the planning and budgetary planning timetables. Your strategy should include:

i) a mission statement (what is your ultimate vision for the event?)

Here is an example mission statement:
To provide a high-profile festival for the community of Anytown and surrounding areas which will satisfy audience requirements and meet the aspirations of the Council and the community.

ii) an audit (of the external/internal environment, existing audiences, potential audiences)

With regard to 'audience building' you will need to research the various social classes within the event catchment area (ie classes A, B, C1, C2, D and E). You will need to find out:
• age
• sex

- occupation
- means of transport
- distance willing to travel to event

As an example of a market research vehicle, ACORN is a consumer classification system available in postcode format to help organisations identify the profile of their audiences and is invaluable when researching audiences for arts events (at the time of writing this publication, the cost of appropriate address labels from this system is £70 per thousand).

iii) analysis (strengths, weaknesses, opportunities and threats – SWOT)

An example SWOT analysis of an event might be:

strengths

- existing loyal event attenders
- good access to site
- ample car parking facilities
- experienced organising staff
- organisation improves every year
- high level of technical management
- good health and safety track record

weaknesses

- no undercover/wet weather facilities on site
- lack of 'branding'
- limited marketing resources
- diverse range of elected members' priorities

opportunities

- could cater for specialist groups
- opportunities to create mailing lists for next year (data capture)
- partnerships with (other) local authorities
- have a 'give 'em what they want' policy
- use the USP (Unique Selling Proposition) of the event, eg type of audiences, size of event, geographical position, welcoming atmosphere, attendance of celebrity/royalty
- use marketing plan to attract sponsorship
- build relationships with relevant agencies such as Regional Arts Boards, etc
- maximisation of secondary income opportunities (sales of souvenir programmes/catering/merchandising)
- introduction of new market sectors

threats

- similar event in neighbouring areas
- other local events with different pricing policies, especially 'free' events
- difficult economic climate (possibly within the organising local authority)

iv) aims and objectives
(as outlined in the Planning Section in Chapter 2)

v) the plan (tactics, budget, sponsorship)
See various chapters relating to these items

vi) implementation
(who does what, when and how)
The strategy should be a working document used by all involved in the event and actioned by all individuals who are allocated specific tasks. The strategy should be monitored, updated and rewritten whenever necessary. The following activities should be paramount:
- programming policy
- pricing levels/structures
- pricing differentials
- incentives
- promotion
- distribution
- daily monitoring of ticket sales (for more information about ticket sales see section on ticketing – Chapter 11 – technical aspects)

Reviewing the event is just as important as planning and implementation. Achievements should be recorded:
- box office income
- secondary income
- grants
- donations
- sponsorship
- customer satisfaction
- audience development
- new markets gained
- staff performance
- on-site management
- pre-event and on-site public relations
- promotion
- monitoring and review (post event – what worked, what could be improved)

> When a dog bites a man, that is not news ...
> but if a man bites a dog – that is news   John B Bogart

chapter six

promotion and publicity

★★★★★

An event is, of course, much easier to promote if it is already established as an important event. If it has a history of being well organised and has a high degree of audience and staff loyalty, this provides an excellent base from which to market your event.

a) publicity tactics

Listed below is a number of tried and tested publicity tactics highlighting a number of marketing opportunities, particularly with regard to promotion, ticket sales and public relations. This list is meant to stimulate the thought processes for maximising sales opportunities, improving public image and to assist in staging a high-profile event.

- Stage a press call with hospitality.
- Ensure programme caters for specialist groups.
- Give out free promotional items in advance to advertise the event.
- Develop relationships with national and local press, radio, television, trade press outside as well as within catchment area.
- Do leaflet drops/mailshots directly to homes (if an envelope is used, sell space in the envelope to a local company who may wish to advertise — this will offset any mailing charges).
- Negotiate eight-page colour pull-out supplement with local newspaper or use the 'wrap around' method.
- Contact TV production companies to create a behind-the-scenes documentary (or produce a storyboard with the same theme for newspapers).
- Engage a high-profile celebrity/crowdpuller to attend press calls, talk to the public about their views on the event.
- Involve a charity with a high-profile patron.
- Use sponsors' names as frequently as possible in publicity material.
- Always use photographs with press releases, they usually attract more attention than text.

- Use local colleges/universities' art departments to design posters/brochures, etc.
- Advertise on taxis and buses.
- Run a competition using the phrase 'using your skill and judgment' (but remember that any special promotions, such as competitions, should last for ninety days only).
- Use display boards in public buildings, eg leisure centre, library, civic centre.
- Persuade shopkeepers to stock brochures and display posters, offer an incentive such as two free tickets to the shopkeeper.
- Link the event to an anniversary.
- Brochure stocks should be held in the tourist information centre, library, local hotels, colleges, doctors and dentists surgeries, hairdressers, restaurants, pubs, schools, etc using a leaflet distribution agency (relatively inexpensive). The agency will ensure that stocks are tidily displayed and replenished at appropriate intervals.
- Erect banners.

b) corporate image

A corporate image creates instant associations in the minds of customers. Every time you communicate with somebody you create an impression of your organisation. Everything you commit to paper therefore will dictate somebody's perception of your event. A clear corporate image for your event will save time, money and effort in addition to generating a greater response to your work. It will ensure a consistent and professional identity to all who come into contact with it.

Everything that is associated with the corporate image for the event should be associated with quality. You can spend less time worrying about what your print job will look like if you work within the corporate image guidelines.

Think about what you want to say, how you are going to present it and how it could be improved. Think about everything you print. Talk to your design team, provide a full brief on how you want your material to look.

Extract from a company's corporate image guidelines

The following is a short extract from an organisation's corporate image guidelines manual. It is a demonstration that consistency, clarity and quality are key when applied to the presentation of a well-organised event:

Logo

Do
- Only use the logo as a piece of artwork. It should not be used as a word(s) in the middle of a sentence or a piece of text.
- Use the colours, sizes and positions as specified.
- Use the logo in colour wherever possible: as part of a print job, on letterhead or on pre-printed paper stock.
- Check with the design team if in any doubt.

Don't
- Distort the logo or rearrange the constituent elements.
- Use the logo too small.
- Use the logo within text.

correspondence

Accuracy, clarity and consistency should be the key elements. A consistent appearance, style and quality is essential to establish and maintain a professional image. Keep correspondence simple, clear and concise. Few people read beyond the first couple of paragraphs in any detail. Even fewer will give a second page a second look.

style

Consistency of written style (how you display dates and numerals, how you spell certain words, etc) will demonstrate that your organisation is working as one entity. Ask yourself:
- how can your message be made most effective?
- does your message fit in with your marketing strategy?
- which print format will be most appropriate to your message and to your audience?

Spelling

Accuracy matters. Spelling errors can quickly erode any impressions of professionalism that you have created. Use the spell-check on your PC; re-read what you print; ask somebody to proof-read before you post; check with a dictionary; take time to get it right.

c) theme

A theme provides a brand for the event and is the most visible aspect of marketing. It can:
- create a high-profile image which is distinctive and memorable
- encourage high levels of participation
- assist in attracting sponsorship, donations and gifts
- raise the profile of an area and its residents.

To make the theme work it must be understood that this is only a part of the whole marketing mix. Organisers will need to ensure that they create a logo which is in line with the theme and which is instantly recognisable. It should be applicable to a wide variety of situations, particularly to publicity material. You must ensure that guidelines for its use are available to everyone who is going to be using the theme and logo as outlined in the previous paragraphs relating to corporate image.

d) media relations

It's all too easy to complain about lack of coverage in the press and other media for our events. We all have it in our hands to improve the situation.

Here are a few pointers worth following to help in dealing with the media. With these suggestions and your own ideas and initiatives, you may have some success in obtaining the coverage your event deserves:

- be professional at all times
- be reliable – send whatever information you promised
- be punctual – deadlines are crucial to journalists
- be accurate – no-one likes to publicise erroneous information
- be friendly – work hard to cultivate relationships with media contacts

- be first – the 'first' of anything is news
- be controversial – the media want 'news', not necessarily 'bad' news
- be well presented – a clear press release, properly presented and issued is essential
- be personal – follow up by phone call to journalists you have circulated if you have further information to give
- be visual – a good picture is worth a lot of words to readers, journalists and sponsors
- be innovative – new ideas are more likely to get coverage
- be interesting – feature the unique, or most novel, aspect of your event in your press release headlines
- be positive and enthusiastic – your attitude will affect that of the media: enthusiasm is infectious

There is no magic remedy or guarantee of success but following these guidelines – thinking them through on each occasion – will help get better coverage.

Remember local media will be keen for your information, but national less so. You have to work harder for the bigger coverage.

Good media coverage adds to an event in many ways – for spectators, officials, sponsors and participants. It makes all the effort worthwhile if many people are interested.

The following are key points in maintaining good media relations and ensuring that media coverage is obtained for events:

- Plan activities well in advance and keep the media informed.
- Make direct contact with the editor and specialist journalists to discuss potential coverage for events.
- Be precise in details provided to the media of future plans.
- Build up stories around personalities, local and national.
- Pick out local elements of national stories for local media outlets.
- Don't be put off if initial attempts at local or national coverage do not succeed – discuss these matters with the editors and be persistent in pursuing them and coming up with new ideas.
- Supply copies of forthcoming events lists to magazines and newsletters which circulate within the media.
- Include photographs whenever possible.
- Don't simply concentrate on specialist features or journalists. Arts, sports or tourism, for example, can justify coverage in general features, as well as news and current affairs slots.
- Be professional in the approach at all times and study the relevant advice and publications to retain up-to-date knowledge of the media and how to approach them.
- Use of other relevant agencies, like Arts Councils or Sports Councils publicity mechanisms, to add to your own.
- Have a recognised event or promotion contact for the media rather than a diverse range of people giving diverse views. The personal touch is very important for all concerned.
- Remember there are many forms of media: all want information so try to utilise them all. There cannot be too much information being pumped into the media to allow them to plan coverage.

Make sure that you provide the media with information and situations with which they can work. The following is a list of tactics which could be used to attract the attention of the media:

- Stage a press call for an event launch. The first exposure for the event should be a press release, sufficiently early to ensure that the information allows time for newspapers, magazines and newsletter deadlines.
- A photocall should be arranged to coincide with this release, featuring performers and the organisers.
- Invitations to the photocall should be restricted to press representatives, key council representatives (if appropriate) and sponsors.
- Staging the press call outdoors will stimulate the interest of passers-by and create some local publicity.
- In order to ensure press coverage, develop human interest stories and features with photographic support.
- Create a co-ordinated publicity programme for the event including the media and advertising.
- Give special emphasis to securing coverage in local and regional media within a thirty-mile radius (if it is a 'local' event).
- Produce an event newsletter.
- Produce a supplement for inclusion in the local newspaper.
- Publicise information about concessionary tickets.

Appreciation is expressed to Regan Cowland Associates who contributed to the information on attracting the attention of the media and also for writing the example press releases which follow. Their details are listed in the back of this book.

e) advertising

Well-targeted, cost-effective advertising can be the difference between success and failure for events. It is also an important matter to consider the costs involved in placing advertisements. You must be clear about your objectives and who your target market is.

There is a wide range of advertising vehicles available, for instance:
- newspapers
- magazines
- newsletters
- poster sites
- buses/taxis
- railway stations
- radio/television
- Ceefax/Teletext
- direct mail (door to door)
- school noticeboards
- surgeries (doctors, dentists, etc)
- cinemas
- underground
- reverse side of car parking tickets
- other public places such as leisure centres, hairdressers, colleges, etc.

The usual types of advertisements appearing in newspapers or magazines take the usual formats:
- wrap-around (local newspaper)
- double-page spread
- full page colour
- full page mono (black and white)
- half page colour
- half page mono
- quarter page colour
- quarter page mono
- spot colour (a single colour added for a small charge)
- classified
- earpiece (usually in the form of a small strip designed diagonally across the corner of a newspaper)

The cheapest form of advertising is if you are successful in persuading the local newspaper to sponsor your community event which usually results in free or very low cost advertising.

f) printed material

brochures
Event brochures should contain:
- the title of the event
- the subject
- who should attend and why
- the intended participants and spectators
- where and when the event will take place (including a map showing how to find the venue)
- the outline programme
- cost, what it covers and payment terms
- how to register, including a registration form or ticket application
- essential administrative details (eg timings, travel and accommodation)
- any special terms and conditions (cancellation charges, discount schemes, etc)
- the name, address and telephone number of the organising body along with the company name, registered number and address. It is also useful to give the VAT number
- disclaimer notice (usually in the form 'the organisers reserve the right to make such changes to the programme as may be necessary due to conditions outside their control')

g) press releases

Journalism has been called 'literature in a hurry' and that analysis will be endorsed 100 per cent by editors who have to sift through mountains of press releases, produce stories and meet deadlines.

Remember, hard-pressed editors have a VERY SHORT attention span. If the first sentence of your press release doesn't grab their attention and give them an idea of what follows on, they will file it in the waste paper bin. It is so important to ensure that your first sentence 'hooks' the editor. If it interests him/her it will probably interest the reader. By providing well written press releases which require the minimum of sub-editing, you are increasing the chances of event news being published or broadcast.

Here are some general rules for putting together press releases. Perhaps you may consider the criteria too involved and detailed but don't forget that this is the newspaper game and you have to play by their rules.

Even if you do follow the guidelines, there is no guarantee your news will be printed but don't give up – keep trying. Editors will always respond to a local news source who submits good, clear copy on time. Establishing a working relationship with the local media will ensure that your event is covered.

Press coverage – why do we want it?
- increases awareness of event
- encourages new participants, spectators, audiences and is fuel to sponsorship
- lets general public know about the event
- assists in attracting sponsorship and general interest
- gives existing sponsors good publicity
- influences funding authority, ie Regional Sports Council or local authority

Setting out a press release
- A4 paper
- typed on one side only where possible
- double-spaced with wide margins
- dated
- event contact name, address and telephone number, e-mail, fax number
- embargo date – which delays publication – if necessary
- make sure it is submitted BEFORE the publication's print deadline

Key points to cover:
- answer the questions who, what, where, when, why and how
- keep length of first sentence to NO MORE THAN 20 words and keep following sentences as short and snappy as possible
- never start press release with words THE, THAT or THIS
- make sure details – dates, names and times – are correct
- don't use flowery language, cliches or jargon
- if copy goes onto further pages, write MORE at bottom of each completed page and END below the last sentence of press release
- NEVER run sentences from one page to the next
- don't underline anything
- be topical

Content
- Always date your press release.
- Don't forget your contact name and number.
- If the editor wants to follow up the story he/she will need

to get back to you quickly. If you have a home and a business number, give both.
- Headlines: the best way to learn to write headlines is to pick up a paper and go through the leadlines in it, looking at the style. Try to think what the essence of your story is and then express it in five words or under. Make your headlines witty, give them some sort of impact They are the first thing which readers will notice, and if your headline doesn't attract their attention they will not read your story.
- have a half- to one-inch margin on either side of the page
- Introduction: once again, if your introduction is not gripping, no one is going to read the rest of the story. As in the case of headlines, try to think of the essence of your article and the most exciting way of presenting it.
- Paragraphs: you must write in paragraphs for newspapers and you must put your paragraphs in order of importance of the subject matters they contain.
- Style: the actual result and an accurate account are of less interest than the human interest story. Put the event into context. Try to get pertinent quotes from key event parties.
- Avoid writing technical details that would baffle the ordinary reader. Write what is termed 'journalese' and is the normal language you see written in reports. Editors do not appreciate flowery English. Journalese crams as much information into the fewest possible words.
- See the following example press releases which received national press coverage.

example of press release

HOLIDAY SPOTS CAN DEFUSE
TOURISTS V RESIDENTS' WAR

Breaking down 'us and them' barriers between tourists and residents is the key to success for Britain's tourist spots, a conference will be told.

Harvey Bailey, Chief Officer for Leisure, Entertainments and Tourism with Weymouth and Portland Borough Council, said the dilemma for resorts "is making visitors feel at home when your residents wish they were!"

His advice comes at a crucial time when the pound's spending power is tempting Britons to holiday abroad rather than book in the UK, causing a slight decline in the domestic holiday market.

Bailey, who addresses Leisure98 the Institute of Leisure and Amenity Management's (ILAM) annual conference at Bournemouth International Centre from June 29-July 2, hopes that Weymouth, at least, has done more than most to make British holidaymakers more welcome all year.

The resort has spent the past decade persuading residents that tourism is a help rather than a hindrance: "There used to be complaints that everything done was for the benefit of tourists and visitors, and the residents had to pay for it," he said.

"Since then, we have done a lot of work to involve the community, so facilities are clearly seen as being there for local people, while events are viewed as community events which are bigger and better than a small town like Weymouth could afford, due to the money brought in by tourists.

"It is a huge psychological barrier to overcome but we have done it."

ends

Shirley Boards or Steve Loader
REGAN COWLAND ASSOCIATES - 01622 684507

Jonathan Ives
ILAM - 01491 874800

FAMILIES IN PARKS AT RISK
FROM 'CHEMICAL WARFARE'

Britain's local councils are using hundreds of tons of pesticides - and much of it in parks where families and their pets could be at risk.

Councils will be warned of the dangers when Mark Davis of the Pesticides Trust addresses Leisure98 - the Institute of Leisure and Amenity Management's (ILAM) annual conference at Bournemouth International Centre from June 29-July 2.

Davis, National Projects Officer for the Trust - a charity concerned with the harmful health and environmental effects of pesticides - said: "Local authorities use 600 to 700 tons of active ingredient a year – considerably more than a decade ago."

"The total includes public health pesticides and herbicides used on roadsides and verges."

Davis said there was an obvious risk that fall-out from this 'chemical warfare' ends up in the water supply and introduces poisons into the wildlife food chain, leading to the loss of species, particularly song birds.

But in parks there is an added risk: "In park areas we are particularly concerned about the exposure of people to pesticides," says Mr Davis.

"Children play there and roll around on the grass which has been sprayed, and people walk their dogs there."

He added that, in an ideal world, no pesticides would be sprayed in public parks, but the Pesticides Trust takes a realistic approach and prefers to work with co-operative councils to promote alternatives where possible.

In conjunction with the Institute of Leisure and Amenity Management (ILAM), the Trust last year launched the Green Flag Park award scheme.

To qualify for this, parks must demonstrate pesticide reduction or elimination strategy and meet a range of stringent criteria: "There is no point awarding a Green Flag to a park just because little or no pesticides were used there if, for example, it had potentially dangerous play equipment," said Davis.

As a result, just seven parks managed by six councils have qualified to fly the Green Flag since the scheme was launched last year. To qualify, parks must be:

- welcoming - with good, safe access to all members of the community

- healthy, safe and secure - with safe play facilities, well controlled dog fouling, with toilets, drinking water and phones, where appropriate

- clean and well maintained - with policies on litter, vandalism and maintenance

- appropriately managed for conservation of wildlife and structural features

- able to demonstrate full community involvement

- marketed as a community resource

more

- managed soundly, following a plan which is regularly reviewed

The award-winning park must also be sustainable - which means maintenance and facilities should be environmentally sound:

- with an environmental policy in place and regularly reviewed

- pesticide use which is minimised and justified

- no use of horticultural peat

- waste plant material must be recycled

- high standards of horticulture and tree care

- measures in place for energy conservation, pollution reduction, waste recycling and resource conservation

It adds up to a tough package, but one welcomed by parks directors and managers, said Davis: "Unlike the Blue Flag scheme for beaches, there is no legal criteria for parks, and they see the Green Flag as the first measurement for quality they have ever had."

"It gives them a yardstick and they acknowledge that the criteria are tough, but they aren't saying lower the standards, they are saying this is the level we must reach."

"Despite the demands of the scheme - which awards a flag and an explanatory plaque for the parks, and the right for the council to display the award symbol on stationery and in marketing - the Pesticides Trust has received 400 expressions of interest so far this year."

"Britain's parks have been badly neglected for years," said Davis. "Parks aren't a statutory service so they have borne the brunt of successive cut-backs."

"The Green Flag Park Award Scheme, launched last year on a shoestring budget with support from the Department of Enterprise, Trade and Regions, is proving to be a major incentive to improve parks. With the continued enthusiasm of park managers and users and sufficient budgets, we hope to make an increasing impact for the benefit of the public and the environment."

ends

16 June 1998

For further information on the ILAM Conference please contact:

Steve Loader - Regan Cowland Associates 01622 681528 (direct line) Jonathan Ives - ILAM 01491 874800

For further information on the particular topic covered by this news release please contact:

Mark Davis - Pesticides Trust 0171 274 8895

h) marketing and promotion checklist

- appoint advertising agency
- compile programme of events
- establish logo
- register logo
- print logo guidelines
- produce competition for mascot
- campaign with direct mail/personal selling, telephone sales
- compile advertising schedule
- produce public relations strategy
- identify opportunities for sales promotion
- consider most economical/effective packaging
- signage schedule for venues
- keep a film and book record of the event
- produce regular event update publicity
- consider commemorative coins/stamps
- consider radio/tv advertising
- produce maps for the event
- order flags and banners
- order merchandising items ie pins, ties, badges, caps, etc
- requirement for medals/certificates for volunteers
- consider hospitality arrangements for sponsors
- are there to be any displays/exhibitions?

> One does not plan and then try to make circumstances fit those plans. One tries to make plans fit the circumstances
>
> General George Patton

chapter seven

health and safety

a) Health and Safety at Work Act

Health and safety is an essential part of quality control, a business with good health and safety controls in place is in all probability a well run, 'quality' business. Unfortunately health and safety management is usually the last consideration for many poorly run outfits and does not even register with the kind of people who arrive on horse back and wear big hats. As a 'rule of thumb' guide, if health and safety is looked after, the rest of the business is usually well run and in order. Quality and health and safety go together hand in hand. They are different sides to the same coin. With a better understanding of health and safety management it will become very obvious as to how quality management and health and safety management are entwined and linked as one. Health and safety is a management responsibility of equal importance to productivity and quality. Effective health and safety management is not 'common sense'. It is based on a common understanding of risks and how to control them. This can only be brought about through good management thus leading to a co-operative effort at all levels in an organisation.

There is a requirement to comply with The Health and Safety at Work Act (HASAWA) in the *The Guide to Health, Safety and Welfare at Pop Concerts and Similar Events* (Pop Code) and in some Public Entertainment Licence conditions but it generally gets overlooked. Worse still, it is often considered that the Pop Code is the same as HASAWA and therefore we need to do no more to meet our legal obligations. Very few suppliers understand their basic responsibilities under the HASAWA, the various regulations it covers or what is legally required of them. These days there is a lot more to health and safety than just seeing that a safety rail is fitted to a stage.

In most cases, the Pop Code sets out the basic standards for health, safety and welfare for people attending concerts,

shows and gigs. The HASAWA sets the basic standards of health and safety that we must achieve during our events (including the set-ups and breakdowns). It is designed for our benefit to maintain our own health, safety and welfare as well as that of the public. The Pop Code is only guidance: the HASAWA is legislation.

There is a very good chance that your insurance company will dump you like a hot potato if any non-compliance with The Health and Safety at Work Act and the various regulations it covers is found during an insurance claim investigation. It is a little like finding your car insurance is invalid after an accident because you do not have an MOT certificate.

Large companies and organisations or those involved in very hazardous operations may, in addition to the information provided in HSE publications and guides, need to consider the use of a health and safety consultant to give them the advice and information they need to help them comply. There are now training companies such as Stagesafe who can provide safety awareness/induction training to both employees and freelancers. Regulation 6 of the HASAWA states that employers must (if required) appoint competent person(s) to assist them with the management of health and safety.

Local authorities are now getting much more concerned about the enforcement of all health and safety regulations. They have a duty to enforce the HASAWA and the regulations it covers in addition to any Public Entertainment Licence conditions. This duty has been passed on to them by the Health and Safety Executive. If they do not enforce the regulations they may be considered to be negligent by a court of law if an accident has taken place, therefore they must enforce the law to cover their own backs.

b) flow of information

If genuine changes are to be made in the way we work and we are brought into line with current legislation, then we need to start with good communication. There is no point in having great ideas without letting everyone else know. Similarly, if you have got something important to say about the way you are working, there needs to be a good flow of information around your company so that everyone can be appraised of a risk or new work practice. See Health and Safety (Consultation with Employees) Regulations 1996.

c) a healthy attitude

We must be aiming for the establishment of what is known as a health and safety culture within the events industry, that is to say, we all think about, consider and communicate with each other on health and safety matters at all times. To make this work and be effective it must be done in a frank and friendly way. Employers must involve their staff in health and safety planning and management systems: health and safety is not a 'bolt on' or an 'added extra'. To be effective it must be 'a way of life' or philosophy.

d) planning for safety

Heath and safety starts at the planning stage for any concert, festival or tour. Production managers/tour managers have a critical role to play throughout. It is normally at this time that a production schedule is drawn up and this needs to be done with health and safety in mind in order to establish what are known as 'safe systems of work'. For example, a 'load out' after a show can be planned so that no one is having to work on stage or can gain access to the stage when riggers are working above. To achieve this successfully, staff, suppliers and contractors must be involved in this health and safety planning.

e) responsibilities

It will become more and more obvious that we all have a large number of responsibilities under the HASAWA. We start first with the venue or site owners who have a

responsibility to make certain that their site or venue is safe and free of hazards for anyone they invite into or onto their premises. They must inform the person that hires the site or venue of any known hazards and they may also have an implied duty to ensure that their client is competent and operating in a safe way according to the HASAWA.

Next come the promoters or performers with whom we work. They have a legal duty under the HASAWA to provide a safe working environment and to ensure that the contractors they appoint are competent and have suitable and adequate health and safety management systems in place. The latter can be done by asking for a copy of a company's health and safety policy statement and copies of any written risk assessments, method statements, records of training, qualifications, etc which can then be checked to see if the proposed controls are considered to be suitable and adequate for the proposed job. This duty will almost certainly fall back onto production/tour managers as they normally book suppliers and contractors.

It is advised that at the same time they request a copy of the contractor's Public Liability/Employers Liability Insurance to see that this is also adequate. Records of this assembled information should be kept.

f) the work environment

It is the employer's responsibility to ensure that the working environment is healthy and safe and that suitable welfare facilities such as toilets, drinking water and First Aid facilities are provided for staff. Employers are required to give staff adequate training and information about the job and details of such training should be recorded as evidence that it has in fact been given. Employers are required to produce a health and safety policy statement and risk assessments for the operations to be carried out. Employers must co-operate on health and safety matters with staff, contractors and anyone else whose health and safety may be affected by their actions.

g) selection of staff and contractors

It is in this area that quality, competence and health and safety are linked the closest. The advice is to have a written set of procedures for selecting staff, contractors and suppliers.

These may include one or more of the following techniques: formal and informal interviews, checks on records of training, experience, qualifications, CVs, references, recommendation, reputation, observation and previous experience of working with that company/person and, if necessary, health and fitness checks. Information and records for individuals should be kept in confidential personnel files. Many local authorities use systems originally designed to cover the Construction (Design and Management) (CDM) Regulations for selecting contractors for their lists of approved contractors. It is normally necessary to be on this list before you get a chance even to supply a quote.

The kind of information normally required is as follows:
- accident records (including RIDDOR) and reporting systems
- risk assessments
- health and safety policy statements (in addition to the basic policy statement this document may include details of the health and safety arrangements the company/business has in place, responsibilities and procedures that help to produce safe work practices and safe systems of work)
- method statements
- details and records of staff training and training schemes operated
- qualifications
- fire and test/inspection certificates for equipment

All this seems to be a lot to ask for but it is now quite normal within most industries to be asked for this kind of evidence. Should a supplier/contractor have a serious accident at the site/venue that a production manager/employer is in charge of, then God help that production manager/employer if they have not checked, recorded and obtained copies of this information from the contractor in question.

All these checks are part of your quality management system. You are responsible for the contractors you appoint and unless you have checked their competence there is no way you can call your business a quality business. You cannot just appoint contractors and 'let them get on with it'.

Any company or business that employs (or is responsible for) five or more people (who may even be self-employed sub-contractors) is required under the HASAWA to have a written policy on health and safety and written risk assessments for the operations they carry out. The policy statement sets out the official policy and arrangements for health and safety within that company or business, and must also state with whom the overall responsibility for health and safety lies. This is normally the proprietor or the managing director. He or she must also sign the policy.

Details of the policy content should be given to all employees so they are aware of the arrangements in place and what is expected of them. The policy statement document may, in addition to the basic policy statement, contain details of procedures and work systems that must be followed, risk assessments, method statements and other information that lead to safe systems of work.

Of course, not all the dangers and hazards may be created by your operations. Often they are created by others working alongside. Employers and those in charge have a duty to inform and warn other workers of these dangers and the safety systems that should be in place to control these dangers. For example, a rigger may drop a lamp from out of the truss on to the head of a backline technician or the PA may get turned full on when you are standing two feet in front of the bass bins and damage your hearing. You should be warned of these dangers and keep records to prove that you received the warning.

Like it or not, this is where some kind of training, backed up by certificates of competence, is so important. They show you have received training and information and that you are aware of your legal responsibilities as well as showing competence in the tasks you have been asked to undertake.

Risk assessments now form much of the basis of modern health and safety thinking and approach and they are used to help create safe systems of work. At its most basic a risk assessment is an analysis of how dangerous a certain situation or activity is, what the likelihood is of an accident occurring and what the implications are of such an occurrence.

We live in an age where parents can sue a theatre for scaring their child with a production of Peter Pan. What are the legal implications for an employer whose workers may be injured by an accident about which they had no prior warning or which they were led to believe was perfectly safe? Even now the courts are deciding on civil claims arising from injuries allegedly sustained through use of a typewriter or keyboard. Just think of the possibilities in the events industry!

h) the risk assessment process

All of us carry out risk assessments everyday without even thinking about it, such as when we cross a busy road or drive a vehicle, but for our purposes of establishing a 'safety culture' we must adopt a more formal approach and record the assessment in writing.

As stated previously, the hazards we are assessing need not be a direct result of your operation: they may be due to other contractors or inherent environmental risks. Either way, the employer/contractor has a duty to identify any significant hazards, carry out an assessment, record the risk assessment in writing and inform his/her staff.

There are many different types of forms available for recording risk assessments. Whatever method is chosen the following points marked *** must be included:

Date of assessment
Name the person making the assessment
Name the job or operation to be assessed (if applicable, or give the brief job description)
Identify and record the hazard *** (The first option should be to remove the hazard or replace it with a safer alternative). These may include:

- fire
- chemicals
- vehicles
- moving machinery parts
- work at height
- noise
- poor light
- weather
- manual handling
- electricity
- work hours

List those at risk and approximate numbers *** (List as groups not by individual name).
These may include:

- members of the public
- artists
- other contractors
- venue staff

What is the likelihood of an accident?
Impossible, remote, possible, probably or likely?
What is the worst possible outcome of an accident?

(Without any controls in place)
equipment damage - no injury
trivial injury
minor injury
major injury
fatal injury

Risk Class
The above information can now help us to class the risk as high, moderate, minor or acceptable.

Information
List your current information available on the hazards such as Codes of Practice, HSE Guidance, Statutory Regulations, British/GEN Standards or Industry Best Practice.

Current controls***
What are the present systems for controlling the risk? These may include training, qualifications, supervision, protective equipment or clothing, written safe systems of work, warning signs, structural calculations, provision of suitable work equipment and certification.
Are the current controls adequate?
Yes or no? If the answer is no:
What further action is required to reduce the risk to an acceptable level?***

List what you need to do to reduce the risk to an acceptable level. The law says you should first of all try to remove the risk but if this is not possible then the next best option should be used. If the risk is classed as 'high' you take cost into consideration when considering what control systems may be suitable.

Give yourself a target date to put any new controls into practice and name the person responsible for doing this. Record all this information on the assessment sheet.

Remember, risk assessment is about what is happening in the workplace not what you think is happening.

On the risk assessment forms under 'information' or 'current controls' one of the following terms is often used:
best industry practice
custom and practice
best practicable means
These terms are fine on a form but a court may not consider them to be 'suitable and adequate' control systems for the risk involved.

Monitoring***
This is one of the most important parts of the process. You must monitor your control systems to see that they are working adequately to control the risks. If they are not working you should review your assessment. Name the person responsible for monitoring controls and reviewing the assessment. All assessments should always be reviewed annually or if work, materials, practices or circumstances otherwise change.

The whole point about these assessments is that they should not just be a 'paper exercise'. To be effective all staff must be involved and the controls continually monitored to see that they are working, this is our health and safety culture in action.

When drawing up your risk assessment, involve the people who will actually be doing the job. This will give them a greater understanding of the needs and reasons behind their work. They may be able to offer ideas and information you may have missed. Give a copy of the finished assessment to these people so that they are aware of the controls in place and can play an active role in the monitoring and controlling.

In the unfortunate event of a serious accident, the first thing an HSE Officer, insurance investigator or court of law will want to see are copies of the risk assessment for the operation. They will then investigate to see which of the controls failed and decide who may be responsible or to blame.

Finally, a lot of people go wrong with risk assessments when trying to cover an entire operation in one single risk assessment. It may need several; manual handling, electrical safety, climbing, flying, trip hazards from cables and leads and so on.

This health and safety section is adapted from An Introduction to Health and Safety Management for the Live Music Industry *written by Chris Hannam of South Western Management and published by the Production Services Association (PSA). ILAM is grateful to Chris and the PSA for allowing this extract to appear in the book and organisers are advised to contact Chris Hannam for more detailed information relating to health and safety matters. Details are listed in the back of this book.*

i) example of a risk assessment chart

RISK ASSESSMENT RECORD

item................................. location.................................. ref.no..

assessment completed by.. date...

activities: (brief description of the operation)

severity	likelihood	risk class
equipment damaged	impossible	high
no injury	remote	moderate
trivial injury	possible	minor
minor injury	probable	acceptable
major injury	likely	
fatal injury		

hazards:

number of persons at risk:

employees: contractors: public:

with no controls:

worst likely outcome: likelihood of occurrence: risk class:

with no controls:

codes of practice

manufactures instructions

industry best practice

HSE guidance and regulations

item.. location... ref.no..

current controls:

adequate control: YES/NO

action plan

action required:

by whom:

target date/time: completion date:

current control to be monitored and assessed by:
and frequency:

j) security and stewarding

The primary duty of all security staff is to ensure the safety, welfare and enjoyment of all customers and others attending an event. Security staff must treat all customers politely and with respect at all times. Staff should be sensitive to customers in distress or difficulty and assist them by refering them to welfare organisations on site when necessary. They must co-operate effectively with others working at the event and care must be taken to ensure that any action by security personnel is proportionate to the situation being dealt with and not to appear aggressive or 'over the top'.

Stewards are there to help rather than control, to make everyone's experience enjoyable.

Stewarding tasks may include:
- controlling parking
- marshalling traffic
- assisting police and other emergency services
- clearing litter
- fire patrolling
- patrolling pit areas in front of stage
- guarding barriers, gangways, exits and entrances
- backstage security
- dealing with minor incidents quickly and effectively with minimum disruption
- stewards must at all times respond quickly when help is required

Stewards should work in teams of six to ten people with one stewarding supervisor per team and one overall Chief Steward. When employing a professional company, make sure that personnel:
- are over the age of eighteen
- are familiar with a code of conduct
- are trained in emergency evacuation procedures and first aid
- wear a distinctive uniform
- carry public liability insurance
- carry a recent photograph for identification purposes
- consist of a mix of both sexes
- reflect the range of ethnic and cultural groups likely to be found among participants
- have an adequate communications system and be trained in its use
- undergo regular training

Responsibilities of the organiser
The event organiser is responsible for proper steward behaviour, in particular:
- the conduct of security staff
- briefing stewards as to their duties
- providing site plans
- providing code words for use in emergency situations
- providing sufficient rest and refreshments between shifts

Searches
Customers and their property may be searched only for a clearly stated reason (ie illicit merchandise or weapons) and where reasonable suspicion exists. Searches may take place at points of entry to the site only, except where requested by the police, and must be confined to property and outer clothing. No customer may be required to remove any items of clothing.

All items searched must be replaced as found and all property treated with due care. People must only be searched by people of the same sex. Children may not be searched. Security staff may not conduct searches for illegal drugs – this is a matter for the police.

The requirements of the law must always be observed. Any search conducted without consent is an unlawful assault. No-one may be required to submit to a search as a condition of being admitted unless this requirement is brought to their attention before they have paid for admission.

Security staff may not confiscate property of any kind and if in doubt should seek the support of the police.

Under no circumstances may security staff take money from the customer except where this is part of their role and is for admission or other fees authorised by the organisers. In all cases where money is taken some form of ticket or receipt specifying the amount paid must be provided, whether asked for or not. Any staff found to be contravening this rule must be removed from the site immediately and appropriate action taken.

Security staff may not carry, display or use weapons of any kind nor may they use force except 'reasonable force' as allowed by law to restrain individuals.

Any person detained by security staff must be immediately reported and handed on to the police.

The charges you would incur may be in the region of £10 per steward per hour, although during millennium year this charge will significantly increase. You may be able to use local volunteer groups for some duties but you should refer to the Pop Code for detailed information on stewarding.

k) welfare services

Welfare is a human service provision which should not be assessed in the same way as goods or structures. It must be arranged on the basis of trust between the parties involved. The primary duty of all welfare staff is to alleviate the distress of people attending the event. They must treat all people politely and with respect at all times and should be sensitive to people in difficulty.

Welfare services at an event can be organised in a variety of different ways. At a small event, a single team may be responsible for the whole range of general welfare. More often, at larger events such as rock concerts, there will be a number of groups providing different services such as:
• information
• counselling
• befriending
• dealing with lost children
• helping people with drug problems
• lost/found property

Every welfare team must ensure as far as possible that the service which it offers is organised and presented so as to be appropriate and accessible to all persons who may be in need of it, and to facilitate equal access to it by all those attending the event, irrespective of age, sex, class parenthood, race, culture, religion or philosophical beliefs, disability or sexual preference. There must be good communications between different welfare services and other providers of services on site, eg the organiser's team, stewards, first aid etc.

It is important to make sure that all welfare services are covered by insurance.

The following are examples of typical welfare services which can be provided:

Information service
People attending events will ask for a wide variety of advice. The following are tips for dealing with typical enquiries

made at an event:
Make a list of addresses and phone numbers of the nearest:
• banks/bureau de change/24 hour cashpoints
• chemists (including duty chemist over weekends)
• police station
• Social Services emergency number
• hospital with casualty department
• 24 hour garages
• bus station
• railway stations (and timetables)
• taxi firms
• bed and breakfast/guest houses
• Calor Gas suppliers
• camping shops
• public telephones

Have available:
• telephone directory
• Yellow Pages
• record cards for recording people's names who cannot find their relatives or friends on site
• maps of the site showing all features, facilities and attractions
• event programme and timings
• name of events manager and how they can be contacted in an emergency

Lost property
Report lost property to lost property office and police

Found property
• keep records (index cards in categories of items)
• do not leave unattended
• do not accept left luggage
• take addresses of people handing in found property so that owner can thank them
• offer advice to report loss of lost credit cards to police and banks
• do not let members of public look in the lost property by themselves for a lost item
• ask for proof of identity and full description of property
• issue a receipt and keep a copy (although this will not be valid in an insurance claim)

Lost/found children
In this instance, lost children includes teenagers under fifteen years of age. Helpers must sign a statement to the effect that they do not have any criminal convictions for offences relating to children.

- remember to look after the parents as well as the children
- in the event of evacuation of the event site, take children with you
- keep a record of their details
- reassure the child
- never leave children unattended
- if you take a child anywhere (ie a visit to the toilet) tell other helpers which child you are taking and where you are going
- alert the Police and security, giving a full description of the child
- be cautious when providing food and drink as the child may have an allergy
- the parent/guardian must sign the record before the child is collected

Penny Mellor is a welfare consultant with many years events experience and the authors wish to express their thanks for this contribution on welfare. Penny's details are listed at the back of this book.

l) insurance

Insurance protection for events is often one of the last things which organisers consider but is an essential ingredient of any event irrespective of size. Specialist insurers are available and can be contacted either directly or through an insurance broker.

Listed below are areas of cover to be considered, some or all of which may be relevant to a particular type of event.

1   Cancellation and abandonment

This type of cover is normally available so that it protects organisers against cancellations or abandoned events due to causes beyond their control although it is not possible to insure against lack of support for an event or financial failures. Examples of problems for event organisers are venues being unavailable at the last minute, bad weather, equipment failure, strikes and power cuts. Indoor events tend to pose less of a problem but with the development of the outdoor event industry in general, our ever-changing weather patterns can provide problems of their own. Organisers of outdoor events should consider the following:

i)   Pluvius (agreed value) cover – if an event is dependent upon admission fees from the public on the day, then even fairly light amounts of rainfall can affect income. Rain is therefore measured during the most important hours as far as the organiser is concerned and, depending on the amount of rain that falls, a claim is made against the sum insured for the event. For example, an organiser whose gate opens at 10am in the morning may wish to insure the hours of 7am to 11am to protect those hours during which most visitors are expected to turn up.

ii)   Abandonment cover (severe adverse weather) – this cover applies to complete or partial cancellation of events but not necessarily due to rainfall. Snow, high winds, hailstorms, fog and a great many other types of weather problems can cause an event to fail and, more specifically, a considerable amount of rainfall on the days leading up to the event can mean that the ground becomes waterlogged and the event has no chance of beginning. In these circumstances insurers will often provide funds to take remedial action (for example, emergency track-way provision) in order to help the event go ahead. It is particularly important that this type of cover is taken out at an early stage, as insurers may be hesitant to provide cover within seven days of an event, particularly if bad weather is forecast!

Events can also be affected by the non-appearance of key celebrities or personnel although, again, remedial action cover will give added protection for alternatives to be provided where necessary.

Cancellation insurance is probably one of the most misunderstood types of insurance cover so organisers should seek advice to find out which type of cover is best for their particular type of event.

2   Equipment insurance

Organisers will often be made responsible for any equipment they hire in addition to their own goods, so it is important that adequate cover is taken out. Many insurers will not ask for an itemised list of equipment because this is not practicable but it is useful to have your own check list in case particular items are stolen. Portable communication equipment often goes missing and some insurers require a separate note of these in any case. For example, make a note of who has been supplied with a handheld radio and keep a note of the serial number. Your insurance should be capable of dealing with losses even where the equipment is only borrowed for a short time.

Many items of equipment are often stolen from events, both indoor and outdoor, so it is important that the insurer is someone who understands the events industry and does not insist upon signs of break-in order to trigger a claim. This type of approach just will not work because often sites are easy pickings for thieves. However, insurers will normally insist upon twenty-four hour security, for outdoor events in particular. Cover for equipment is usually offered on an 'all risks' basis so it includes accidental damage in addition to theft. Organisers will normally be responsible for the first £250 of any loss. If responsibility is taken for transit of items to and from an event, then this should also be insured.

3   Public liability

This is a very common form of insurance and is well known to many people. It deals with the organiser's legal liability for damage to property and death or bodily injury to third party persons. Even the slightest injury can often result in organisers being contacted by a claimant's solicitor and therefore this cover should always form part of the insurance package for an event. Members of the public can be seriously injured or even killed at events but it is also important to include legal liability cover for any participants in activity days or similar being organised. Just because a group of people is raising money for charity on the day, it does not mean an organiser is safe from legal action. Often an indemnity of £1,000,000 is the norm but venues may request higher limits in order to satisfy their own contract conditions. Higher amounts are easily available and it is not expensive to satisfy the demands of venues or local authorities.

4   Employer's liability

When taking on either direct labour or even unpaid helpers, it is important to make sure they are covered in case of injury while working under the direction of the organiser. Back injury claims are not unknown even when a helper has only put in a few hours to assist with the event!

5   Personal cover for participants

Accidents can occur even though there is no allegation of negligence, so organisers may consider providing a package of benefits for each participant (similar to travel insurance) so that they can claim individually should they, for example, be off work due to an accident on the day. For £1 or so per person, per day, this cover is well worthwhile.

Depending on the type of event, there may be other areas to consider but organisers should find that the above provides a good basis for successful insurance arrangements.

For further details on events insurance, contact Steve Warner at Insurex Expo-Sure Limited who provided this advice on insurance. Details are contained at the back of this book.

legislation

Always remember that there can be legal differences between the countries of the United Kingdom, especially England and Scotland; there can also be specific local authority and byelaw differences.

It is always worth checking the details with appropriate local officials and enforcement agencies.

This chapter is only a simple guide and neither the author nor the publishers can be held responsible for its total accuracy or for any errors.

Sponsorship is the hardest part of all

Robin Knox-Johnson

chapter eight

sponsorship

The most intriguing thing about the quote at the start of this chapter is not the statement itself but the speaker. It would be expected that sailing round the world single-handed is a significantly difficult task but Knox-Johnson suggests that finding the sponsorship was the hardest part of the work he undertook. This speaks volumes about the sheer difficulty in obtaining sponsorship for any project, no matter how worthwhile.

There are, however, some golden rules well worth following for those seeking support. A proper approach to obtaining sponsorship will aid, but never guarantee, success. There have been occasions in the past when individuals have almost stumbled on sponsorship support and this probably will continue to happen in the future but it becomes less likely as businesses become more hard-nosed about the returns they expect from any sponsorship package. They have clear ideas about what they want and they will assess any sponsorship deal on its ability to deliver to their requirements.

The day of 'charitable donations' of sizeable amounts of money to a perceived good cause to run events or follow through promotions on just personal whim or sympathy are diminishing if not disappearing.

Finding sponsorship is hard work and event organisers should recognise it as such, allocating time or specific individuals to undertake that work as for other tasks within the organisational structure.

Checking off your approach to sponsorship against some of the attached checklists will help guide you in the right direction. It is essential that the information from these lists is taken and moulded appropriately to specific situations as not all the issues considered will be relevant every single time; nor is any such guide ever totally comprehensive and some issues may have been omitted.

Sponsorship is best defined as a 'mutually beneficial business arrangement between sponsor and sponsored to achieve defined objectives'. This definition is apt and identifies a number of vital criteria. It is important that everybody recognises that:

- there are benefits to both parties and these should be agreed

- the defined objectives of each party should be identified and understood by each other

- sponsorship must have something in it for everyone as everyone wants something out of it

There will have to be a close match of stated objectives if the sponsorship arrangement is going to be sustained and successful.

a) sponsorship proposal

A professional approach must be taken to seeking appropriate sponsors and a sponsorship proposal should be drawn up and presented to potential sponsors.

The proposal should include the following headings:
- title of event, date and place
- contact name of the organiser (or sponsorship officer)
- duration of event for which sponsorship is sought
- the theme, corporate image and branding to be used (especially on publicity material)
- quantify amount of publicity material to be used which should in turn reflect the total amount of exposure available to the sponsor
- target market/potential audience
- anticipated ticket sales

- names of other sponsors
- arrangements for a press launch
- opportunities for sponsor to supply a message or for advertising opportunities in publicity material
- types and frequency of press releases
- opportunities for speeches by the sponsor and meeting of other VIPs

It is wise NOT to include the amount of sponsorship sought at this stage if cash is required. It is not professional to go 'cap in hand' asking for a specific amount of money and indeed this can be very off-putting for a sponsor. The proposal should first of all attract the attention of a potential sponsor and arrangements should then be made for a meeting and presentation. Ask the sponsor if they have a budget in mind. The proposal can then be tailored to meet the budget if necessary. Sponsorship in kind can be included in the proposal.

b) potential problem areas

Like so many things, sponsorship is great if it works but difficult to disastrous if it doesn't. Beware of potential problems and keep on top of them.

- Mismatching: arising out of the difference in ambitions or view between the sponsor and the sponsored, or conflicting aims, ambitions and targets.
- Misunderstanding: this often arises from the lack of a clear explanation of what both parties are about and hope to get out of the arrangement.
- Deception: this can be due to the sponsorship-seeking agency not accurately representing what they can actually deliver and trying to 'con' the sponsor.
- Non-delivery of benefits: again related to what can practically be delivered and being unrealistic can eventually result in the non-delivery of previously promised services.
- Withdrawal of sponsors funds: it is possible that due to changing business circumstances that a sponsor may withdraw their support with or without good reason. This is one reason why a written agreement is absolutely vital.
- Change of image: if something happens to change the image from positive to negative then the sponsor may be upset and wish to withdraw from a potentially negative association.
- Cancellation: cancellation of an event can spell disaster for all concerned and really major sponsorship should not

be taken on for an event which is liable to cancellation, without a clear understanding of this possibility by all concerned.
- Misadventure: if something negative takes place during the event, for example an accident, injury or violence, this can cause major embarrassment for all concerned and damage sponsorship relations.
- Specialist advice: both parties should take outside advice before becoming involved in a sponsorship agreement if they are inexperienced in this area.
- Insurance: each party should consider covering cancellation risks, major catastrophies or losses from their side of the deal.

c) a written agreement

A written agreement for the sponsorship is now essential for all concerned. While it need not be a lengthy legal document for smaller events, include at least the following items:
- the identity of the parties involved
- what particular role the parties are contracting to undertake
- a definition of the rights and benefits to each party
- a definition of exclusivity of rights or benefits
- identification of who is responsible for the delivery of these rights and benefits
- how and when payment is to be made
- the protection of ownership of names, logos, emblems, etc relating to the event
- the provision for the termination of the sponsorship contracting as a result of default on either side
- provision for event cancellation
- provision for alterations in sponsorship agreement if the value of the event changes dramatically, eg television coverage is either added or withdrawn

d) VAT on sponsorship and donations

'Sponsorship' is the general term used for financial or other support, such as the giving of goods or services by businesses to sport, the arts, the educational sector and other businesses.

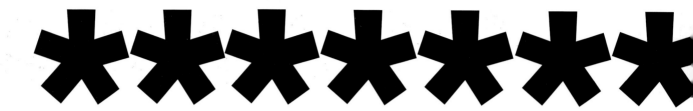

If something is supplied to a sponsor in return for the sponsorship then a taxable supply is made. It does not matter how the sponsorship is described; what counts is the reality of the terms under which it is provided. If the sponsorship is provided on condition that clearly identifiable benefits are supplied in return (such as publicising the sponsor's business or products or making facilities available to the sponsor) VAT must be accounted for on everything received under the sponsorship agreement.

The publicity may be, for example:
- an event, concert or display named after the sponsor
- the sponsor's name being incorporated in the name of a team or of a team's horses, or displayed on a team's vehicles or shirts

If, on the other hand, nothing is done or given in return for the sponsor's support, a taxable supply is not made and the sponsorship can be treated as outside the scope of VAT.

However, to be treated as outside the scope, the sponsor's support must be entirely voluntary and must secure nothing whatever in return. If the only acknowledgment of the sponsor's support is a simple mention in a programme or annual report and nothing else is required, it is still outside the scope. If a contribution is made on condition that the sponsor's name or trading style is advertised or promoted, or that the sponsor receives some sort of benefit (such as 'free' tickets, beneficial booking rights or a 'free' advertising slot in the programme), then it is consideration for a taxable supply and VAT must be accounted for on it.

If a sponsor gives a donation in addition to providing sponsorship under an agreement, the donation can be excluded from the amount on which VAT is accounted for provided that:
- it is clear that the donation is entirely separate from the sponsorship; and
- the amount of sponsorship is realistic in relation to the benefits provided to the sponsor.

Clearly, if benefits are provided to the sponsor on condition that the sponsor gives the donation, it is part of the consideration for the supply and must be included in the amount on which VAT is accounted.

Donation of goods

True donations of services or money are outside the scope of VAT. Gifts (donations) of goods from registered donors must be accounted for by the donor on the cost of the gift (unless the cost is £15 or less). If the gift is used for the purposes of the business, VAT can be reclaimed as input tax subject to the normal conditions.

Newspaper and magazine competitions

Publishers of newspapers or magazines who run competitions for which prizes are donated may have a general understanding that the donor will benefit from some publicity as a result. However, provided there is no specific contractual obligation to provide advertising or publicity in return, there is no supply of advertising to the donor and therefore no need to account for any VAT. The donor would treat the supply of the prize(s) as a business gift. But if there is a clear contract under which the donor provides the prize on condition that advertising is provided, a taxable supply is made to the donor, and again, you must account for VAT. Furthermore, if the donor is registered for VAT, he or she must account for VAT on the open market value of the prize(s).

Value for VAT purposes

VAT must normally be accounted for on everything received under a sponsorship agreement, including anything which is distributed as prizes, paid over as expenses or secures benefits for the sponsor. Where goods or services are received from the sponsor in return for services under the terms of the sponsorship agreement, this is a form of barter and there are two separate supplies. The sponsor must account for VAT on the value of the goods or services supplied and the recipient of the sponsorship must account for VAT on the open market value of the services supplied to the sponsor. This will normally be equivalent to the value of the goods or services received from the sponsor.

Where the agreement provides that the amount of money to be paid by the sponsor depends, for example, on the success of the sponsorship, VAT must be accounted for on the actual amount received.

VAT registered sponsors must be issued with a tax invoice for the amount on which VAT is accounted. The sponsor can then reclaim the VAT as input tax, subject to the normal rules. If the amount agreed makes no reference to VAT it must be treated as VAT inclusive, unless a separate charge for VAT is made.

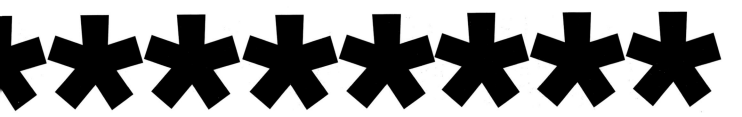

Sponsorship for non-business activities
Sponsorship for something which is not by way of business may be treated as outside the scope of VAT unless supplied on such a scale that it constitutes a business in its own right.

Agents
The VAT treatment of sponsorship is the same whether or not either party employs an agent. An agent must account for VAT on any commission received.

Overseas sponsorship
Supplies involving advertising and publicity rights to overseas sponsors may qualify for zero-rating. If you enter into any 'unusual' sponsorship agreement not clearly covered by the above, you are advised to consult with your VAT office.

Public authorities
Goods and services supplied to government departments, local authorities, embassies, foreign missions and international organisations in the UK are taxable in the usual way and tax invoices must be issued.

Certain goods and services, supplied by government departments and local authorities will be taxable and tax invoices will be issued in the usual way.

Croner's Reference Book for VAT *provides excellent financial advice on sponsorship and the authors' thanks are extended to Croner's for agreeing to the section on VAT on sponsorship being reproduced. Further details on Croner's Reference Book for VAT can be found at the back of this book.*

e) sources of information for sponsorship

- Yellow Pages
- newspapers
- business rates register
- business organisations
- professionals
- participants
- library
- market research
- past partners
- existing sponsors

sponsors might support an event for:
- community awareness
- public awareness
- low-cost promotion
- media interest
- publicity
- competitive advantage
- association
- promotional campaign
- customer/client entertainment
- event exposure
- commercial benefit
- image
- public good
- donation
- target audience
- corporate relations
- reflected glory
- marketing tool
- personal interest
- philanthropy

f) sponsorship in summary

According to recent research, world-wide sponsorship expenditure is estimated at £15 billion, growing six times faster than advertising.

An implicit part of the planning process will be your strategy for attracting sponsorship. When you set your event objectives, you will need a clear idea of your target audience.

If you have a likely sponsor in mind, think about who the sponsor's target audience is and try to tailor your event to this specific audience. Spend time researching your sponsor. You may even want to create an event specially for a particular company. Some sponsors demand exclusivity and will not have anything to do with events which are sponsored by a number of organisations.

Some large companies have been unable to find an event that suits their customers and have created their own events. Carlsberg, for instance, created its own rock concert targeting an audience with an age range of 18 to 24. As well as not being able to find an existing event to suit them, they also felt that sponsoring someone else's event did not give them total control of marketing, nor did it maximise brand impact. Now their event attracts 72,000 people.

Persuade your would-be sponsors that your product can be flexible. Ask them to join you in the early planning stages and give them some ownership of the event. They will want to see a marketing plan and will want to be assured that you are spending both time and finance on publicising the event. They may want hospitality and free tickets, or to be included in photocalls, press launches and so on. Do not forget to ask them what they want in return for their sponsorship and do not assume that you (or even they) know exactly what they want. You are responsible for their payback. Make sure they get it because they will want a return on their investment and you will want them to come back next year.

You need to build long-term relationships with your sponsors.

When seeking and working with sponsors:

do
- have a clear idea of your target audience
- make your product flexible
- get your sponsors on board in the early planning stages, invite them onto the team
- keep sponsors involved all the way through the planning stages, during the event and planning for future years
- create a marketing plan (including costs)
- clarify with your sponsors what they want from you in return for their support
- build long-term relationships with sponsors
- make sure you know the rules on VAT on sponsorship monies
- treat sponsors as VIPs at the event they are sponsoring and all the time

don't
- specify initially the amount of money you are looking for wait until the sponsor is ready to tell you how much exactly they can provide
- make promises you can't keep
- take the money and run

If there were no bad people there would be no good lawyers

Charles Dickens

chapter nine
legal

a) duty of care

Leisure managers are under increasing pressure to maximise the use of their facilities by providing a wider range of special events for both visitors and local communities.

The diversity of such events – from fairs to festivals, competitions to concerts – brings many different management and operational problems, not least of which is the safety of those visiting and participating. It is, therefore, of crucial importance that managers responsible for such events are aware of their legal and duty of care responsibilities.

A common law duty of care underpins the statutory responsibilities of those who stage special events and the Occupiers' Liability Acts of 1957 and 1984 assume great importance.

All who participate in any event, sport or recreation, amateur or professional, run the risk of injury. Lawyers have the task of distinguishing between those injuries the participant must accept as an 'occupational hazard' and those which may qualify for financial compensation.

The person responsible could be a fellow participant (in the case of sport) or an organiser of an event. In most civil claims for damages it is alleged that someone was 'negligent'. The law of negligence states that damages must be paid by A to B where it is proved A owed a 'duty of care' to B not to injure B, that A was in breach of that duty of care and B suffered injury as a result. The court must assess whether a duty of care exists, not always a foregone conclusion. To establish a duty of care situation a plaintiff must prove the defendant acted recklessly or carelessly.

The managers/organisers of recreational events and leisure activities owe a duty of care to users, participants and visitors in their capacity as organisers and occupiers of the premises or facilities concerned. Under the 1957 Occupiers' Liability Act, an occupier of premises used for leisure activities must take reasonable care to ensure there are no hidden dangers, that equipment is fit for its purpose, that there is adequate supervision and that routine safety checks are undertaken.

The duty of care may be modified by an express term in a contract with a user of the premises, or an organiser may purport to exclude liability by the prominent display of a notice to that effect. However, occupiers cannot exclude all liability for injury, loss or damage since such exclusion is illegal under the 1977 Unfair Contract Terms Act.

The Act of 1957 does not deal with trespassers. However, an occupier also owes a duty of care to trespassers or those who 'gate crash' events under the Occupiers' Liability Act 1984. Prosecution may result if it can be proven an occupier was aware that a trespasser was in the vicinity of danger when he/she was injured.

The 1957 Act also deals with an occupier's responsibility to users who are children and states that an occupier must be prepared for children to be less careful than adults.

Under the 1982 Supply of Goods and Services Act, it is implied into a contract for the supply of a service that a supplier will carry out the service with reasonable care and skill.

If an event or a leisure facility is closed for a period of time for essential maintenance by a contractor or events organiser, then the contractor/organiser could legally be in occupation of the premises for that period and therefore be responsible for duty of care in relation to visitors. Similarly, a contractor employed by a local authority to manage an event has legal occupation and is therefore responsible for duty of care to users and visitors to that event.

A court will evaluate many factors and assess whether a defendant has complied with common law and contractual and statutory obligations. By following prevention guidelines and adopting appropriate risk management strategies, injuries due to an unsafe event or equipment can be reduced to a minimum. It is even possible that insurance premiums can be reduced as a result.

The 1957 Occupiers' Liability Act is of importance to all who work in public leisure services. Any doubt about responsibilities under the Acts should be referred to a legal advisor but the basic principles are based on simple common sense, reason and foresight.

For example, an organiser is responsible for ensuring that an adequate level of stewarding is provided at key points of the venue. The number of stewards used should be based on a comprehensive assessment (see section on Stewarding – Chapter 6).

Demand for events will continue, so it is important that those responsible for their management are fully aware of their roles and responsibilities and acquire the skills necessary to ensure a safe and enjoyable event.

The above section was written by Nick Reeves during his employment as Director of Policy and Information at ILAM.

b) legislation

The Heath And Safety At Work Act (HASAWA) is an umbrella act, which covers a great number of regulations, most of which apply to all companies and services that make up our industry. These regulations include:
• The Noise at Work Regulations
• The Health and Safety (First Aid) Regulations
• The Reporting of Injuries, Diseases and Dangerous Occurrences Regulations (RIDDOR)
• The Electricity at Work Regulations
• The Control of Substances Hazardous to Health Regulations (COSHH)
• The Lifting Plant and Equipment Regulations
• The Workplace (Health, Safety and Welfare) Regulations**
• The Management of Health and Safety Regulations**
• The Health and Safety (Consultation with Employees) Regulations 1996
• Personal Protective Equipment Regulations**

• Provision and Use of Work Equipment Regulations**
• The Manual Handling Operations Regulations**
• The Display Screen Equipment Regulations**
• The Consultation with Employees Regulations
• The Health and Safety (Signs and Signals) Regulations
• The Firework (Safety) Regulations 1996

The Health and Safety Executive can provide you with free leaflets, books (priced) and other easy-to-follow guidance on all of the above regulations and related subjects. Six of the most important regulations (marked**) are European Directives and are covered in a set of six guidance books known as The Six Pack.

Companies and businesses are advised to consult HSE books for details of the literature available and to obtain copies of The Six Pack and other relevant publications. Ignorance is no excuse and will not get you off the hook if you should be unfortunate enough to run into trouble.

The guidance on Legislation is an extract from An Introduction to Health and Safety Management for the Live Music Industry *written by Chris Hannam of South Western Management and published by the Production Services Association (PSA). Chris is an expert on health and safety issues and his address and that of the PSA are included in the listings 'Helpful Organisations' in Chapter Thirteen.*

c) licensing

Experienced event organisers will perhaps realise that with regard to entertainment licenses, there is a lack of consistency between licensing authorities. Not only do licensing terms and conditions vary enormously between local authorities, but also the cost of a license varies, ranging from £100 to £5000. Those organisers who stage many annual events are working to persuade various licensing authorities to compile a standard scale of charges so that organisers know what to expect for each event.

For the purposes of demonstrating the types of conditions which may apply, an extract has been used from the licensing documentation of West Berkshire Council as follows:

These are a collection of standard conditions which may apply when a council issues a license for:
a)   The performance of a play by virtue of the Theatres

Act 1968

b) A Public Entertainment by virtue of the Local Government (Miscellaneous Provisions) Act 1982 for:
i) music, dancing or entertainments of a like kind - or
ii) sporting events to which the public are invited as spectators – or
iii) musical entertainments held mainly in the open air

c) A private entertainment licence for dancing, music or similar entertainments to which the Private Places of Entertainment (Licencing Act) 1967 applies.

Definitions

For the purpose of these conditions the following definitions apply:

- 'Air supported structure' means a structure that has a space-enclosing, single-skin membrane anchored to the ground and kept in tension by internal air pressure that it can support applied loading. The membrane may or may not be restrained by trans-surface ropes or cables.
- 'Approval/approved' means approved by the council in writing.
- 'Attendant(s)' means an adult whose duties include the supervision of the audience to assist the licensee.
- 'Audience' includes all persons invited to attend a licensed function.
- 'British Standards' (BS) includes British Standards Codes of Practice and Specifications issued by the British Standards Institution.
- 'Building' includes a temporary or movable building and also includes a permanent or temporary structure and any vessels remaining moored or on dry land.

- Competent person for the purposes of this license must be for inspecting electrical installations/equipment
  i) a Corporate Member of the Institute of Electrical Engineers
  ii) a contractor enrolled with the National Inspection Council for Electrical Installation Contracting
  iii) a suitably qualified representative of the supply authority
  iv) any other person deemed competent, with prior approval of the council

For inspecting as installations/equipment:
Member of the Confederation for Registration of Gas Installers (CORGI)

For inspecting liquified petroleum gas LPG installations/equipment:

An engineer from either the installation company or the manufacturers of the equipment

- 'Durably flame-retarded fabric/scenery' means fabric/scenery that has been chemically treated to render it flame-retardant so that when subjected to the appropriate wetting or cleansing procedure of British Standard 5651 it retains a stated performance when tested to British Standard 5438 Tests 2A and 2B with a 10 second flame application time in each case.

- 'Emergency lighting' means lighting provided for use when the supply to the normal lighting fails.

- 'Flame-retardant fabric' means a fabric which meets the performance requirements of British Standard 5867: Part 2: Type B and retains this performance after being subjected to the appropriate wetting or cleansing procedure in British Standard 5651.

- 'Hypnosis' includes mesmerism or any similar act or process which produces or is intended to produce any form of induced sleep or trance in which the susceptability of the mind to suggestion is increased or intended to be increased.

- 'IEE Regulations for Electrical Installations' means the current edition of the Regulations for Electrical Installations published by the Institution of Electircal Engineers (IEE).

- 'Licence' means the document issued by the council giving permission to the licensee to hold either a performance of a play, public entertainment or private entertainment. The license document shall comprise all the conditions specified and any special conditions.

- 'Licensee' means the person or persons to whom a current license has been granted.

- 'Log book' means the book kept and maintained by the licensee to record any test results, etc as required by the conditions.

- 'Means of escape' is the structural means whereby a safe route is provided for persons to travel from any point in a building to a place of safety, without outside assistance.

- 'Normal lighting' means all permanently installed electric lighting operating from the normal supply, which in the absence of adequate daylight is intended for use during the whole time that the premises are occupied.

- 'Permitted' means permitted by the Council in writing.

- 'Place' of safety means a place in which a person is no longer in danger from fire.

- 'Place(s)' of entertainment means such places to which people resort, including places of recreation, whether as members of the public, members of a club or otherwise.

- 'Pneumatic' structure means a structure or a substantial part thereof, which depends upon air pressure to maintain shape and includes:
  a double wall enclosing membrane or
  a flexible frame giving support to the enclosing membrane, which in each case is inflated to provide shape and stability to the structure.

- 'Premises' means a place, an enclosure, a building or that part of a building within a place including services or installations used in connection with assembly.

- 'Prior' approval means information submitted in writing to the council at least 28 days before the event, for approval and agreement by the council.

- 'Prior notice' means written notice to the council at least 28 days before the event.

- 'Prior consent' means consent in writing from the council in advance of the event.

- 'Special effect(s)' includes any real flame, pyrotechnic, explosive, flammable substance, firearm, replica firearm, smoke, vapour effect, laser, strobe or similar lighting effect.

- 'Stage' means that part of the premises which is constructed or arranged for the performance of stage plays or entertainments of the like kind.

- 'Structure' includes a tent, a pneumatic structure or an air supported structure.

- 'Temporary structure' means a structure which is designed, constructed and erected in such a way that it may be moved from the site either whole or after being dismantled.

- 'The public' means people resorting to places of entertainment and recreation, whether or not they are members of a club irrespective of payment. It includes audiences, performers, contractors and other people who have a legal right to be present on the premises.

Duties of licensee

- The licensee shall at all times be present at the premises during an entertainment. He shall not engage in any activity which in any way detracts from his supervision of the premises and the observance of any license conditions. The licensee shall take all precautions to ensure the safety of the public and shall retain control over all parts of the premises.
- Before admitting any audience the licensee shall inspect his premises to ensure compliance with all license conditions. In particular he should ensure that all exits are properly signed, properly lit and that emergency doors are operational. The licensee shall undertake tests ...and make all necessary entries in the log book.
- The licensee shall maintain good order at all times and shall monitor the audience numbers. The licensee must at all times maintain an approved method to ensure that the permitted audience numbers are not exceeded.
- The licensee shall ensure that no noise comes from the licensed premises. Similarly, no vibration shall be transmitted through the structure of the licensed premises which gives rise to annoyance to the occupiers of premises in the vicinity. The council may if they think fit apply noise levels to ensure compliance with this condition. Any such condition will be endorsed on the license.
- There shall be on duty at the premises during the whole time that the audience is present, a staff of attendants instructed by the licensee as to their duties in the event of fire or similar emergency. The instructions given to attendants should aim to avoid panic and to supervise the evacuation of the premises.
- Attendants must not engage in any functions which will hinder the discharge of their duties in the event of an emergency or would entail their absence from the floor or tier where they are on duty as attendants.
- Prior notice shall be given to the council of any entertainment intended wholly or mainly for children. The council may impose additional conditions intended to deal with such entertainment, in particular relating to the number of attendants. Any such additional conditions shall be endorsed upon the license.
- The licensee shall ensure that the premises are not used

for any special effects without the prior approval of the council
- The licensee shall ensure that toilets for the audience shall be available for use
- The toilets shall be kept in a clean and well maintained condition
- All wash hand basins shall be provided with a supply of hot and cold running water, soap, a suitable means of drying hands and, if necessary, waste bins.

Temporary structures
- Site selection and access
- The licensee shall consider the following factors when selecting a site for the erection of a tent, marquee or similar temporary structure:
  a) access and egress for the public and performers, emergency vehicles and equipment
  b) the proximity of surrounding buildings and vegetation and other fire risks in relation to the spread of fire
  c) the need for a telephone to call the emergency services
  d) the availability or unevenness of the ground
- The licensee shall prepare and submit for prior approval of the council a scale drawing of the proposed site and of any structures on the site. The drawing shall show the position of all entrances and exits, generators, car parking and similar features.
- The licensee shall ensure that the site is arranged so as to allow for adequate means of access by fire fighting appliances to within 50 metres of any part of the structure. Access routes should be not less than 4 metres wide, should have no overhead structure or cable less than 4.5 metres above the ground and should be capable of taking the weight (about 12.5 tons) of fire fighting appliances in all weathers. Emergency vehicle routes within the site should be kept clear of obstruction at all times.

Other sections contained within these terms and conditions include:
- access and means of escape for disabled people: plans, wheelchairs, evacuation in emergency
- fire prevention and means of escape: means of escape, exits and exit lighting, emergency lighting, surfaces and materials, general fire requirements
- seating and gangways: seating sizes, gangways, handrails, seating layout
- tented structures
- floors and tiers

- exit routes
- exit and directional signs
- electrical and gas safety
- lighting

Open air concerts and similar events
- The licensee shall submit for prior approval scale drawings to the council showing:
  a) the position of the site in relation to surrounding roads, residential areas, schools, hospitals or other potentially noise sensitive areas
  b) the layout of the site showing:
  car parking areas
  camping areas
  access gates, perimeter roads and roads within the site
  stage and auditorium positions
  sanitary accommodation, positions and drinking water positions
  maintained clear routes into the site for emergency use
  any other information relevant to the proposals or that may be requested by the council
- The licensee shall submit for prior approval to the council, information in respect of the following items:
  a) the anticipated audience numbers
  b) the names of performers and a schedule of events
  c) details of security personnel and other attendants
  d) provision of fire fighting equipment
  e) means of calling the emergency services

Safety
- The licensee shall meet all fire precaution requirements in relation to temporary structures
- All temporary buildings, tented structures, stages, lighting rigs and any other structures in connection with the event shall be positioned, constructed and maintained to be:
  a) fire resistant to the satisfaction of the council
  b) structurally sound and not liable to collapse in the event of settlement, wind damage, crowd movement or other reasonably foreseeable cause
  c) electrically safe
  d) otherwise safe for its intended use
- The licensee shall provide suitable and sufficient crowd barriers and other physical measures to the satisfaction of the council to minimise dangers arising from audience movement. Similarly the licensee shall provide adequate numbers of attendants and security personnel to maintain good order.

- No special effects shall be used as any part of the entertainment without the approval of the council. The licensee shall not permit any entertainment, exhibition or display involving knives, firearms or replica firearms.

Welfare

- The Licensee shall provide in locations to the approval of the council:
  a) Sanitary accommodation in accordance with the standard laid down in Appendix 3. The sanitary accommodation provided shall be maintained in good working order and kept clean at all times.
  b) Wholesome supplies of drinking water
  c) Disposal facilities for waste water and litter

Noise control

- Generally the licensee shall undertake all reasonable measures to control noise from the event. He shall in particular:
  a) exercise control at all times the level of amplification from performers
  b) be able to stop the entertainment in the event of an emergency or if permitted time restrictions are exceeded
- The licensee shall, if required by the council, appoint acoustic consultants or experts of similar standing at his expense to:
  i) act on behalf of the licensee to represent his interests in terms of noise control and to liaise with officers of the council on matters of noise control
  ii) undertake sound level readings prior to the event, during rehearsals or sound checks and during the event itself
  iii) provide technical advice to the licensee on the measures necessary to control noise from the event
- The council shall impose such conditions as it feels appropriate to control noise. In particular the council may impose noise conditions to:
  a) control the permitted times of entertainments
  b) establish measurement monitoring points
  c) set sound level limits in relation to particular monitoring points and during particular times

Thanks are due to West Berkshire Council for allowing this extract from their licensing documentation.

Phonographic Performance Ltd (PPL)

Who needs a PPL License?
- Anyone playing recorded music in public. Examples include discotheques, pubs, clubs, hotels, restaurants, shops, leisure centres and dance and fitness instructors.
- Anyone who supplies equipment or records produced under PPL's licence for public performance. Examples include background music equipment suppliers and jukebox operators

Playing PPL members' records in public without a licence is an infringement of copyright. It is also illegal to copy sound records and PPL has to pursue anyone found to be making copies of records for a subsequent public performance. Penalties for copyright infringement include High Court injunctions to prevent further use of records or the award of damages, which can be expensive.

PPL is a non-profit-making company set up by the record industry to grant licences to anyone who wants to play records, tapes or CDs in public. People do not always understand that the possession of records, tapes or CDs does not give the automatic right to broadcast or play them in public. Copyright law protects recorded music and this makes it possible for musicians and record makers to receive payment for their work when it is played.

License fees vary according to usage and there are tariffs to cover the whole range of uses. Where appropriate, these tariffs are negotiated with the relevant national organisations representing the different music users.

A PRS licence allows you to use all types of music from all over the world – legally. Whether the music is live or played on a tape or CD player, jukebox, radio, video, TV or karaoke and whether or not the performers are paid, a PRS licence is a legal requirement.

PRS Public Performance licences are required by premises which use music. These range from concert halls and dance halls through public houses, hotels and restaurants to ships, aircraft, hairdressers, doctors and dentists waiting rooms and even telephone 'holding' systems. A PRS licence is usually reassessed annually and is referred to as a 'blanket' licence.

The law states that if you wish to use copyright music in public, you must first get permission from every single writer or composer whose music you intend to use; 'in public' means broadly anywhere outside your domestic circle. However, it is obvious that making such individual arrangements for licences would be virtually impossible, thus the PRS deals with this for you.

PRS will work out the charge for your particular premises using the appropriate tariff for your business and will explain the charges to you.

At the time of going to press, the Minister of State at the Home Office had announced a formal review of licensing laws. It is expected that the review will take at least eighteen months. Event organisers are advised to keep themselves aware of any new legislation concerning licensing laws.

d) contracts with agents

It is important to understand that when you contact an entertainment agency on the telephone and agree to book an artiste, that this is a binding verbal agreement which would stand up in a court of law.

Each agency will have their own performance conditions as every artiste performs for different timeslots, ie some 30 minutes, some 45 minutes, etc. Make sure that you see a copy of their performance conditions before signing a contract. It is usual for performers' food, accommodation, travelling expenses, etc to be included in the contract and you should make sure that this is so.

You will need to fully brief the agent regarding the type of audience you expect to attend, ie gender, age range and numbers. You will also need to provide full information regarding the venue at which the performance will take place, eg indoor/outdoor, purpose built theatre, green field site with full stage facilities, sports centre, etc. Some entertainers will not perform in sports centres or outdoors and it is essential that the agent is fully aware of the type of venue that is being considered. The agent must know what power supply there is at the venue, ie single-phase, three-phase. If no power is available, generators would need to be hired.

Expenditure can be greatly reduced if a purpose-built venue is to be used, with proper dressing rooms, catering facilities and sound and lighting systems. If the venue is not purpose-built or is a temporary structure where Portacabins or marquees are to be used, it can be extremely expensive

to create the infrastructure for the event, particularly when the star of the show demands their own dressing room, toilet and catering facilities.

A standard contract outlines all the terms and conditions and it can be expensive to have it checked by a solicitor, so make sure that the solicitor is experienced at working within the entertainments/music industry.

The following clauses taken from a typical contract show the thought processes you may go through when scrutinizing contracts:

Clause:
The artiste reserves the right, if they have chart success before or on the contracted play date, to renegotiate the fee.
Response:
Addition to clause: ... to renegotiate the fee providing that no tickets have been sold for the performance on (date of event). (Organiser - please note: tickets sold to customers who wish to see a particular performer form a contract between the organiser and the customer, and the non-appearance of the expected performer will result in a breach of that contract).

Clause:
All financial settlement to take place with (artiste) by (date).
Response:
It is typical that you have to pay in advance, especially for a famous act, and particularly for the year 2000 as agencies are now asking for a 50% deposit. If the event does not take place the artiste will expect the agent to pay their full fee.

Clause:
Venue to provide a selection of sandwiches, mineral water, soft drinks and beers.
Response:
Ask agent to be prescriptive about quantities and frequency of catering. If there is a large number of performers, such as an orchestra, with a rehearsal and performance spaning a whole day or more, the volume of catering could significantly increase the organiser's costs.

Some agents do not include any clause relating to cancellation by an artiste. Those that do, undertake to supply another performer "of a similar calibre". Frequently it is impossible to replace the contracted artiste of the same calibre (eg Shirley Bassey, Billy Connolly, Phil Collins, etc) with a performer who would satisfy the customer who has contracted with the organiser to see that particular artiste.

It is advisable to discuss this point with the agent at the outset of your negotiations and to ensure that the organiser has insurance cover in place for cancellation by artistes or for any other reason resulting in cancellation of the event.

The Complete Talent Agency (CTA) have provided advice and information for this section on contracting with Agents. More information about CTA is listed at the back of this book.

e) byelaws

It is impossible to be too specific about byelaws as they are by their very nature local. For every event organiser, however, one thing is certain – there will be a number of byelaws which potentially affect any event.
They concern many issues including:
• street trading
• opening hours
• licensing
• drinking in public places
• dog fouling
• litter
• public performance
• road closures

It is essential that you check with your local council to see which ones affect you – there *will* be some. It is also worth checking with your local police force.

Please remember that byelaws change from time to time, so it is always advisable for event organisers to keep the situation under review in case new byelaws are introduced during the planning stages.

Such byelaws can be quite quirky and in the UK there are several legal and political systems in operation. For example, Scots law and English law can be quite different and allowances must be made for this.

f) legal differences in the UK

Whenever dealing with events (or indeed any other) legislation, it is vital to remember that we are operating in the United Kingdom; each of the constituent countries (and sometimes local authorities) can have different laws and regulations. It is always worth checking with local lawyers and experts. The variances (eg in licensing laws) can be significant and have a major impact on events.

In particular, the differences between English and Scots law are large and to treat them as the same is a big mistake. Historically and right through to the present day, legislation on a whole variety of civil and criminal matters have quite different legal implications. As far as events are concerned, these could include:
• street trading
• drinking in public
• selling tickets
• licensing laws
• powers of local authorities
• police powers

All these and others must be checked on every occasion. Failure to adhere to the appropriate legislation could render the event organiser liable to prosecution.

There's no problem so big or complicated
that it can't be run away from   Anon

chapter ten

infrastructure

a) venue

Size is a governing factor when deciding on a venue. There
is nothing so off-putting at an event as people shuffling
around cheek by jowl. Conversely, it is just as depressing a
sight to have a cavernous room echoing with the sound of
one or two voices.

Do be sure that the venue matches your, and your guests',
expectations in terms of size, location and facilities.

If you have chosen an outside location and/or you are obliged
to provide facilities for your guests, be absolutely sure that
you have selected a supplier that has the capability to carry
out your wishes, is adequately insured and can demonstrate
a track record of success.

The following two checklists cover aspects to be covered
when checking an indoor and an outdoor venue:

i) ILAM Services Indoor List

Name of Venue ....

Address ....

Contact...

Telephone..

Fax ....

E-Mail ....

1. Venue

Is the venue easy to find?....................................

Near to railway station? ....

Car parking available? ....

Distance from airport?...

Map/hotel brochures available? ....

2. Attitude of Staff

Reception:...

Porters:..

Others (specify):..

3. Meeting Room

Name of room: ....

Maximum Capacity - theatre ( ) classroom ( )
boardroom ( )

Are there pillars/mirrors to obstruct/distract?.......

Can the room be partitioned?...............................

Is there likely to be another meeting beyond the
partition?..

Is the partition soundproofing good?.....................

Natural daylight? ....

Adequate blackout?...

Is a platform necessary (is it provided by venue
and included in cost)? ....

Where should the platform be placed?..................

Is platform furniture available? ....

Is baize available to cover tables?........................

Are floral decorations included in hire price? ....

Audio/Visual

Flipchart and pens?...

35mm slide projector? ....

Overhead projector? ....

Size and number of screens? ....

Single/dual projection?...

Cine? ....

Video (television or screen projection)? ....

Laser pointer? ....

PA system? ....

Microphones - top table ( ) lectern ( ) neck/tie
clip microphone ( ) roving microphone ( ) ?.......

Tapes? ....

Technician available? ....

Additional power points?..

Lights - where is control box, can lights be
dimmed?...

Low/high ceiling?...

Heating/air conditioning -
is it noisy in operation? ....

Are seats comfortable?..

How many chairs are available? ....

Banners - yes/no (fireproofed)? ....

Is there likely to be noise from nearby
kitchen/works/traffic? ....

Fire exits? ....

4. Registration

Suitable area? ....

Table/chairs available? ....

Baize to cover table? ....

Telephone point?..

Cloakroom/coat rail?..

5. Catering

Name of room: ....

Close to/same level as meeting room?.................

Maximum capacity - seated ( ) standing ( ) ?......

Table layout - rounds 8/10/12?...........................

Number of serving points -
coffee/tea ( ) lunch ( ) ?.....................................

Speed of service - seated/hot lunch?....................

Good choice of menus?...

Table plan/table identification?..............................

Bar available? ....

Method of payment? ....

6. Facilities

Number of/location of toilets? ....
Cleanliness? ....
Location of public telephones? ....
Shops? ....

7. Workshop/breakout rooms

Name(s): ....
Location(s): ....
Maximum capacity - theatre ( ) classroom ( )
boardroom ( ) ? ....
Audio/visual required? ....
Flipchart and pens? ....
Room for speakers/slide preparation, etc? ....

8. Bedrooms

Single/double/twin: ....
Size of room/bathroom: ....
Checking in/out time: ....
Minibar? ....
Hairdryer/trouser press? ....
Tea/coffee facilities? ....
Desk/table? ....
Lighting? ....
Fire exit instructions? ....
Noise? ....
Breakfast - served in: (   ) times (   )
extra charge for full English breakfast (   ) ? ....
Separate room required: ....
Name of room: ....

9. General

Conference office: ....
Access, eg lifts: ....
Signposting - necessary? ....
Directional signposts available? ....
Posters can/cannot be displayed? ....
Blutack/Velcro can/cannot be used? ....
Details for main venue board? ....
Refurbishment work taking place, if so, when? .....
Cancellation charges? ....
Itemised bill for a residential course? ....
Licenses? ....

ii) NOEA Check List for Site Inspections

THE NATIONAL
OUTDOOR EVENTS
ASSOCIATION

CHECK LIST FOR INSPECTION OF SITE AND FACILITIES

date...

site address ....   organisers ....
....
....
....
....

personnel present at inspection...

1. invitation or ticket arrangements ....
2. public access to and from..
3. fire appliance access ....
4. nearest fire appliance ....
5. policing...   contract...
6. general condition of site...
....
....
....
....

7. bases of structures ....
8. structure stability   stage...
                               grandstand...
                               towers ....
9. fire precautions...extinguishers...............................
10. emergency exits...   visible..
11. first aid facility ....   visible..

12. catering facility ....   hygiene.....................................   access...........................
13. control of beverages ....   alcohol ....
14. other items..
....
signed..   inspecting officer ....witness

Thanks are due to the National Outdoor Events Association (NOEA) for allowing us to use their Check List for Inspection of Site and Facilities. NOEA's information is contained in the listings at the back of this book.

b) fencing

When organising large-scale events, the provision of a perimeter fence may be a factor for consideration.

How can you control who gets into your event on your terms if the venue has public access and no natural forms of segregation?

Sites such as Knebworth, Roundhay Park, and Balloch Castle and Country Park offer the ideal outdoor location for major events and pop concerts but they all suffer the same problem. Being open to the public and literally open or exposed from all sides, the only way to keep the non-paying public outside is to fence yourself in.

By erecting a perimeter fence, usually about 2.5m to 3m high, you can channel the flow of people to turnstiles and entrance gates where they show a valid ticket or pay on entry, where appropriate, and so control site access.

The level of security you require at an event would determine the type of fence that you would use.

Demarcation

For simple demarcation of an area, the common mesh panel fencing is ideal. Providing a clearly visible barrier, the mesh panel system does not block out the proceedings completely and so allows would-be visitors to see what is going on beyond the fence position.

Security fencing

The provision of a security fencing system is common at major events and concerts where the need to restrict and control access is a key factor. To put this into context, the Glastonbury Festival site has a 6.5m high security perimeter fence. This solid fence system blocks the site from the view of those outside and enables strict control over those entering the site. Supported from within the site itself, this system is very difficult to defeat. Security fencing can also combine 'look-out' towers for site security to monitor both sides of the fence.

Combinations of the demarcation and security fence are also common place. By using both systems, a "dry moat" can be created from where security patrols can monitor the outside situation.

Diversification

The same products used to create the high security fence can also be used for other purposes. Such applications vary from temporary roadways, acoustic barriers, secure compounds and even giant speaker boxes.

Temporary road surfaces at events – guaranteed access

Of the major items that are considered when planning and organising an outdoor event, a temporary road surface should rank highly in any serious organiser's priorities.

Often the unsung hero of many events, the temporary roadway is the first product on site and last away, working hard to ensure the event infrastructure has guaranteed access and that visitors enjoy the safety and comfort that a firm surface underfoot provides.

With the right support from the earliest stage of your event planning, you can make the most of a very versatile product. By involving suppliers with many years of experience in providing the answers to your access problems, supplier credibility leaves more time for the finer details that make the difference between another event and a successful one. Using a temporary roadway is more than just protecting the ground; it's about protecting your reputation!

The protection of the underlying ground at outdoor events is sometimes overlooked or the 're-instatement' option taken. However, once the integrity of that ground is damaged, it can be years before the ground returns to the condition that it was in before the event took place. Notwithstanding such environmental damage, the high risk of vehicle damage and the often-expensive insurance claims that follow, should be reason enough to at least consider some form of temporary roadway. Remember – protection is always better than cure !

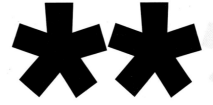

c) barriers

Any event drawing moderate to large crowds needs a safe and controlled environment and there are many ways of achieving this.

Outside events may not offer a natural control mechanism and so organisers will turn to suppliers of temporary barriers. Applications vary from simple demarcation of a specific area to the full force of a Heavy Duty Crush Barrier for segregation and control of large numbers of people.

Used at major events by the Metropolitan Police the 5' Heavy Duty Crush Barrier is the safest and most sturdy type available but other types exist for the many different kinds of events that take place throughout the year. Below are details of the most common barriers available for your event.

Technical specifications

drawing 1

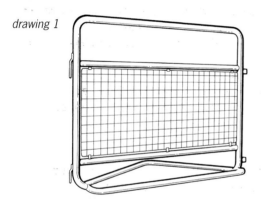

Heavy Duty Crush Barrier

Length: 1.5m
Height: 1.066m
Weight: 27Kg
Finish: galvanised to British Standard 729

All welded construction using 33.7 OD x 3.2 steel tube, with 50mm x 50mm steel mesh panel held in position by six welded lugs. Steel spikes are fitted to the underside of the base frame to prevent sliding.

drawing 2

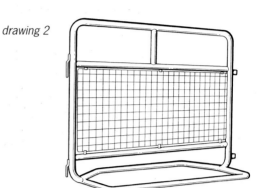

Lightweight Portable Crush Barrier

Length: 1.82m
Height: 1.066m
Weight: 21Kg
Finish: galvanised to British Standard 729

All welded construction using 26.9 OD x 3.2 steel tube, with 50mm x 50mm steel mesh panel held in position by six welded lugs.

drawing 3

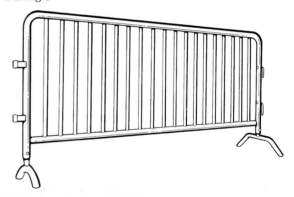

G.T. Lightweight Portable Barrier

Length: 2.59m
Height: 1.0m, 1.22m with feet
Weight: 17Kg
Finish: galvanised to British Standard 729

All welded construction with bolt on replaceable feet. 31.8mm x 2.6mm ERW steel tube to outer frame with 12.7mm x 1.2mm ERW steel tube vertical infill bars.

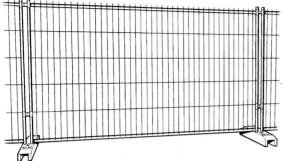

Temporary Fence Panel System

Manufactured from heavy-duty, full-welded, open-mesh panels which are welded to tubular steel frames. Legs are provided at the base of each panel unit to fit securely into a portable solid rubber base. All fence units are finished in a hot-dip galvanise. Panels are available in a standard size of 3.5m x 2.0m high. Accessories such as pedestrian and vehicle gates make for a highly flexible system.

drawing 5

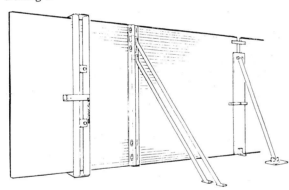

Fortress Fencing

Manufactured from heat-extruded, aluminium planks connected by interlocking, captive-tongue and groove joints. Fortress fencing is available in standard panel sizes of 3.05m wide x 2.6m long that can be coupled simply and quickly. Fortress fencing is a modular system which allows it to be utilised in any location. Transportation, installation and dismantling all need to be carried out by experienced fencing engineers.

Eve Trakway is the main contributor to the sections on Barriers and Fencing and their advice is very much appreciated. Further information about Eve Trakway can be found at the back of this book.

d) Toilets

Whatever happens, try to avoid the 'queuing for the loos' scenario. There is existing guidance from the *Guide to Health, Safety and Welfare at Pop Concerts* which sets out guidelines for sanitary accommodation provision.

Organisers should ensure that adequate sanitary conveniences are provided for the number of people expected and that consideration is given to their location, access, construction and signage. They should not be situated in the vicinity of food stands.

To minimise crowding and queuing problems, sanitary conveniences should, where possible, be located at different points around the venue rather than concentrated in a small area. In deciding on the location, the need for access for servicing and emptying should be taken into account. Portable, no-mains toilets are fine for long-term use providing that they are serviced properly.

Numbers of conveniences required will depend on the type of event. Clearly one where heavy alcohol consumption or camping is to take place will demand a higher number of conveniences. These figures assume a 50:50 male/female split:

Female conveniences: 1 WC for 100 females
Male conveniences: 1 WC for 100 or fewer males
2 WCs for 101-500 males
3 WCs for 501-1000 males

The above figures assume an event duration of eight hours. They may be reduced in the following way for shorter concerts:

Duration of event	Percentage of above standard
More than 8 hours	100%
6 hours	80%
4 hours	75%

It is recommended that a wash hand basin should be provided per WC.

These are guidelines only.

ILAM is grateful to the Hire Association Europe (HAE) for providing this material. These are guidelines only and have been compiled by Portable Sanitation Europe (PSE) which is a member of the HAE. Further details on both the HAE and PSE are listed in the back of the book. The PSE were kind enough to provide the information on toilet provision.

e) banners

There is an increasing need for the external PVC promotional banner when it is correctly manufactured, sized, styled, coloured, 'graphicked' and sited. This can be a very cost-effective method of advertising but how much do we know or need to know when purchasing one or more of these versatile message carriers?

There are two main types of PVC material: supported and non-supported. This has nothing to do with the way they are hung but relates to whether the PVC has a material substrate or not. If there is a substrate, then it is referred to by its weight in grams per square metre (gsm). If there is no substrate it is referred to by its micron thickness, eg 350 microns.

Strength is the relevant factor in tear resistance. Supported is stronger than non-supported and the heavier the better. For one-day shows and throw-away banners you can use an economy grade, say 400 gsm.

For banners that require longer use or that will be subjected to windy conditions you will need a heavier grade, say 550 gsm. The proper use for non-supported PVC is internal sites and positions where they do not come under any strain. Ensure that banner makers use the correct type of PVC for the job in hand.

Some materials are often not suitable because the PVC was not specifically formulated for banner use, so you could find that screen printing or vinyl lettering will not adhere to the surface satisfactorily.

The manufacture of banners is carried out in two ways. One is with welded seams and the other is with stitching. Both ways are effective but stitching leaves a flatter hem which perhaps looks better.

How do you hang your banner? Eyelets are favourite which allow you to pass rope through the holes or cable ties, thus supporting your banner.

The washer for the eyelet should have raised teeth so that when compressed into the banner the teeth grip the material substrate, helping to prevent the eyelet being pulled out under strain. Pole pockets is another method and the size of the sleeve in the banner is dependent on the size of the pole.

Rope can be sewn into the seam which is useful if the banner is to be strung high up or between buildings. If used across a road then wire rope should be utilised for safety's sake.

If you want your banner seen from both sides, then you need a special banner material called Total Block. This has a light blocker built into the material so that you do not get ghosting from the message on the other side. Colour is something to consider. Most people have standard white but why? Professional banner makers hold a stock of standard colours which, when used correctly, can add much power to the impact of your messages. In fact, dual background colour, eg one half yellow and the other black or other combinations, is being pioneered to great success.

What to put on your banner? Text can be signwritten, or more usually vinyled utilising specially formulated banner vinyl, to ensure excellent results. Vinyl will adhere to the flexible surface, weather the elements and will also endure the physical rolling and unrolling of the banner on many occasions to no ill-effect.

The thing to remember is impact. A short, sharp, punchy slogan in a large and clear typeface that can be seen from a distance is bound to be better than a fussy, illegible and overcrowded message.

If you are considering ten or more banners with the same message, then screenprinting is usually the more cost-effective route to take. Whatever method you use you must ensure that the banner is going to be properly and efficiently put into place. What gives the banner a bad reputation is poor hanging.

The banner must be taut and then it will display its message and your company's image to the most effect. One of the best ways is on a specially manufactured banner frame.

Taking care of your banner is easy. If it has vinyl applied then make sure the banner is rolled back onto a tube with the graphics on the outside. This helps the vinyl not to pucker. Above all, make sure the banner is put away dry, otherwise it could deteriorate.

The shape of things to come

A very exciting way of making point of sale messages stick comes in the shape of Boldscan's new Banneret Kits. Not only is the concept a great idea, it is one that really works too. Banneret offers everyone the chance to produce banners themselves instantly for very little cost and also the opportunity to make good profits.

Aimed primarily at the indoor promotions market this lightweight, unsupported PVC material is strong and tear-resistant. A Banneret starter kit comprises of ten metres of white PVC in a choice of widths. You can cut the material to any shape and use it in the standard rectangular form or trim the PVC into any shape. As long as you position grommets suitably so it hangs well, you can produce some interesting, attention-grabbing banners.

Have you ever wanted to position a banner inside a window and had nowhere to tie it to? Well in this situation the Banneret grommets are designed to accept some clear plastic window suckers. This adds tremendous scope to the creativity and the versatility of banners.

Also available is a range of freestanding and lamp post aluminium banner frames.

If you want more advice or help concerning banners than is provided here by Boldscan Banners and Frames, their information is contained in the Resource pages at the back of this book.

f) signage

One of the most important factors in organising your event is to ensure that your visitors find your venue with ease. How do you go about ensuring your road signs are in the right places and will stay there? There are two options:

Option 1 – Arrange and complete the tack yourself. You need to do the following:
- complete a survey of the area and decide what routes your visitors will use
- taking into account the local authority's policy towards temporary road signs, draw up a schedule of locations for road signs
- the schedule must specify the exact fixing point including the number of the lamp column, the size of the sign and the layout
- make sure that your schedule complies with all legal requirements for road sign design and fixing
- approach the local authority with a detailed planning application and ask for their permission to erect the signs

- indemnify the local authority against any incident arising from your signs
- arrange public liability insurance for signs with cover for at least £2million for any single incident
- liaise with the local authority to ensure that, where possible, permission is granted with enough time for you to have the signs made, negotiating legal points where necessary
- once permission is granted, make the signs to legal standards of reflectivity, lettering size, colour and design
- within an agreed timeframe, erect the signs in the approved locations, ensuring they are securely and safely mounted without damaging the post, and fixed to laid down requirements of height and distance from the road edge
- while erecting signs ensure that you are complying with Safety at Street Works Act for work on the highway
- while signs are in position, be able to return to each location to remedy any problems arising that are notified by the police and/or local authority
- within 48 hours of the event finishing, return to the signs and remove them, once again complying with the Safety at Street Works Act for working on the highway
- store or destroy the signs

Option 2 – The Automobile Association will undertake all of this work for you. An 'average event' (if there is such a thing) involves the use of about fifteen signs and for budgeting purposes, organisers should allow approximately £450 plus VAT for the service. The AA will examine the requirements of each event and will charge a price which reflects the work involved.

The AA Signs department is not a profit-making concern but is a service which covers operating costs only. Thanks are due to the AA for providing the information on signage. More information on AA signs can be obtained from the listing at the back of the book.

g) catering

Nearly all events involve catering services to some degree. How should an organiser start planning the provision of catering services? Catering is probably one of the most important aspects of any event. If the food and drink is good, the event is a success (so say the participants!).

The first consideration is that of identifying needs. To do that the organiser needs a clear idea of the nature of the event that they are organising. The factors affecting need include:

- How many people might attend?
- What is the duration of their visit likely to be and how far might they have travelled prior to arriving?
- How close is the event to existing catering outlets?
- Does the programme for the event include specific breaks for refreshments?
- Are there special needs to provide catering for sponsors, sponsor's guests, VIPs, staff, volunteers or performers?
- Is catering included in the admission price?

Satisfying *needs* is a minimum requirement.

The assembly of people at an event also offers a range of commercial opportunities which might be exploited. Some events will require the event organisers to benefit financially to a substantial degree from the catering. Other types of events will provide an income from catering to the organisers – but it is the caterers who stand to benefit most financially from exploiting the opportunities available.

Such is the range of catering requirements at an event that you may need the services of a local voluntary group such as the Women's Institute, a one-person operator with a hot-dog van or the specialist events division of the largest catering companies in the country such as Compass or Gardner Merchant.

There is a clear distinction between seeking caterers to provide opportunistic catering services such as hot dog stalls, beer tents and ice cream at an event and seeking a caterer to cater for your specific requirements such as meals for conference delegates/sponsors guests, free hospitality bars, etc.

The difference is primarily that in the first case 'the event caterers' are selling their produce to the people at the event and taking the financial risk, therefore they must

decide whether there will be sufficient trade for them to cover their costs and make a profit.

In the second case, which we will call 'the outside caterer', the caterer is selling services that you have pre-ordered. They know in advance the services, standards and quantities that are required and the price that has been agreed for these services.

'The Event Caterer'

Factors affecting the *opportunities* include those affecting need:

- Of the people attending, how much might they spend on catering products and what type of products are they likely to purchase? Are people likely to bring their own refreshments?
- During the event, will the people attending be free to purchase catering services at any time or only at certain times?
- Over what period must the service be provided? What are the get-in and get-out times?
- How extensive will the competition from other catering services be? Are exclusive concessions available for particular products or services? Are there opportunities for combining the provision of a service with sponsorship of the event. What licenses or regulations will be required?
- What utility services are available and what site constraints exist?
- How much equipment is going to be required to prepare, produce and serve catering products and, therefore, what is the financial risk to the caterer?
- What happened last year?

The *opportunity* dimension of the catering at an event is something that caterers themselves will be able to judge provided they have good information about the event. The organiser will need to be able to summarise that information on a fact sheet at an early stage. It is an essential tool in making approaches to caterers where the organiser seeks to profit from attracting caterers to an event. That process will vary according to the type of event and could consist of:

- Advertising the catering rights for all aspects of the event in return for a fee. The organiser will detail not only particulars of the event but will also need to specify the minimum services to be provided. It is important not to over-specify as this might reduce the financial return to the organiser. Bids will have to be compared, references may need to be taken up and checks made with

Environmental Health Officers. A presentation may also be requested before deciding on the best bid, ie the one that confirms a good price with an expectation of an appropriate quality of service. Only the largest events, often involving more than one day, are suitable for this process. A formal contract is required. The contract may be renewable for future years. Terms of payment will be specified. If a variable basis based on an element of income share is used, then it must be possible for the organiser to check on the amount due.

- Offering concessions at the event for particular products, eg hot dogs or ice cream. The organiser needs to take care to ensure that if a concession is offered, that it is enforced during the event. Others must know of this concession so that they do not sell something they should not (especially events with voluntary organisations or stall-holders) and traders without a concession need to be dealt with during the event at an early stage. The agreement need only be a simple one. The cost of the concession needs to be specified and the payment arrangements (preferably in advance or on the day) made clear. The arrangement may for example be per ice cream outlet, leaving the caterer free to decide how many outlets to be brought onto the site. Bids could be invited for concessions. Some voluntary bodies may want to offer their services.

- Remember that for outdoor community events it may be necessary to install coolers, fridges, microwaves, etc which will require the identification of power and water supplies; cross reference with power supply/generators

Typical catering checklist for an outdoor sports event:

Special guests – sponsors, VIPs, civic guests
- Private refreshment facilities with a service appropriate to the time of day and duration of attendance.
- Attended service to serve food and drinks and clear, on an ongoing basis throughout the event.
- Check: any presence required of sponsors' refreshment products?

Officials, first-aiders, stewards, etc
- Conveniently situated refreshment services with a service appropriate to the time of day and period of duty.
- Identify items that are free, eg tea and sandwiches. Items that are available to purchase, eg wrapped confectionary; items that are not to be supplied, eg alcoholic drinks.
- May need to be associated with rest area and people

may need space to eat on their own.
- Refreshment tickets/identification needed.
- Special needs, eg cold drinks in hot conditions.

Competitors
- Similar to above
- Some events may include team teas, event dinners or similar. Entry fees may be inclusive of refreshments, eg childrens drinks and snacks
- Special check: eating and drinking times relative to participation in event, special requirements such as drinks during an event.

Spectators
- Range of sales points appropriate to the time of day and duration of attendance.
- Special check: licensing regulations, possible rules of event restricting services, eg no alcohol or no glasses. Are there times in the programme when catering services will be in peak demand?

'The outside caterer'
When an outside caterer for your event is required, some careful research is needed to ensure that you appoint the appropriate type of caterer for your requirements.
Where to start looking for caterers?
- directories
- trade associations lists, eg MOCA (see section on MOCA at the end of this section)
- *Yellow Pages* and similar publications such as *Caterer* and *Corporate Entertainment*
- recommendation

Carry out on a check on the companies which you identify.

For instance, undertake a telephone 'audit' to find out if the catering company answers the telephone promptly, puts the call through to someone who can answer all of your questions and offers to have a meeting to discuss all your requirements. The manner in which they deal with your enquiry will give you a good idea of their customer/client care policy

In order to brief your caterers adequately, consider the following points and questions:
- How many covers can they cope with?
- State the time of day or night the event takes place.
- Provide details of the venue. Is there a kitchen available for preparation of food or will portable kitchens need to

be brought in? Do they need to hire tables and chairs?
- Are your clear about get-in and get-out times?
- Let them know what your exact budget is and ask what kind of meal you can expect for your money.
- Who provides the menus?
- Make sure that they are aware of any special guests and whether special arrangements need to be made for them, eg if the meal is a buffet, you may not wish to have your special guests standing in a queue and would need a reserved table with waiter/waitress service.
- State the composition of the group of special guests.
- Can they adequately cater for special dietary requirements at short notice?
- It should be ascertained as far in advance as possible whether the guests have any special dietary requirements. However, if this information is not available at the time of ordering your meal, make an allowance of 25% of the total covers to be vegetarian food and 5% for vegans. Other more specialised requirements should also be discussed as soon as these are known.
- Will table gifts be provided. If so, to whom?
- It is essential that you determine the type of cutlery and crockery to be used. Costs are dramatically reduced for disposable plates, cups and cutlery but seriously detracts from the quality of the meal.
- The style of service should be determined in advance. What is required?
  - silver service
  - waiter/waitress service
  - buffet - stand up
  - buffet - seated
  - buffet - finger

Remember to prepare the copy for your invitations well in advance remembering to include the date, time, place and dress code.

The event will run far more smoothly if stewards are on site to direct guests to the correct room or reception in advance of the meal.

The following is a checklist of items which you may wish to consider when compiling your catering plan:
- after-dinner speakers
- toastmaster
- top table protocol
- call to dinner
- pre-dinner receptions
- pre-dinner drinks
- cloakrooms
- caterers: ask for examples of similar events references - also from any sub-contractors
- staff resources
- own equipment
- responsibility for missing or broken items
- insurance
- financial arrangements
- floral decorations
- colour themes
- menus
- venue (marquee, etc)
- greeting and seating
- car parking
- performers/entertainers
- physical requirements
- rehearsal time
- dressing rooms
- master of ceremonies
- refreshments
- arrival times
- sound checks
- technical requirements
- contact day before
- welcome on arrival
- check fifteen minutes before if ready to go on
- payment

Appreciation is recorded to Mike Fulford of Leisure Advice for contributing to the section on catering. Mike is also a Principal Consultant with ILAM Services Limited and his address can be found at the back of this book.

The Mobile and Outside Caterers Association (GB) Ltd
Mobile and Outside Catering is generally accepted as a High Risk Activity, usually due to the large number of people provided for.

For several years The Mobile and Outside Caterers Association (GB) Limited (MOCA) has been striving to improve standards within the industry with the introduction of a Due Diligence System in 1992 plus MOCA Safe Food Level 1 and 2 Training Courses in 1995.

MOCA continues to work closely with Environmental Health Departments and other national bodies and is committed to promote and improve food and general safety within the industry.

MOCA aims to provide general guidance and basic standards for caterers operating from mobile trailers, marquees and market stalls in addition to those providing sandwich and buffet services and portable/mobile bars.

The general principle can be applied to both caterers themselves and those wishing to employ the services of catering companies in almost any situation, from a roadside sandwich bar to a show/event caterer and a mobile buffet service working from fixed kitchen premises.

The Code is a voluntarily accepted document and is based on 'good practice' but where there are legal requirements it will be clearly stated.

MOCA recognises and accepts the need for a positive attitude to health, safety and hygiene throughout its membership and the industry in general. In doing so it will take all necessary steps to assist and encourage members to manage their food businesses to the highest possible standard.

In order to achieve the objectives of its policy statement, the Association will:
- co-operate fully with all enforcement authorities to achieve high-quality food safety management
- encourage and facilitate suitable training of all food handlers to appropriate levels of skill and knowledge
- encourage and assist members to work closely with the relevant enforcement authorities to secure for themselves a safe food business

There are differing levels of membership. Members wishing to join to a level other than the basic entry membership undertake annually a diagnostic survey of their food handling arrangements known as their 'Annual Declaration', in addition to agreeing to random inspections and the use of the MOCA Due Diligence system. Guidance, appropriate to the needs of the membership, is given to ensure that good hygiene and safety practices are employed where food is prepared, handled, stored, transported and sold.
In particular, members will be routinely required to:

- in all ways comply with all current legislation
- identify and appropriately monitor all temperature controlled appliances, and take immediate remedial action in the event of operational failure
- ensure that all surfaces are restored to their original state of cleanliness as soon as practicable after use
- maintain an orderly system of stock rotation, ensuring that all food in storage is used in its proper turn and does not become misplaced
- take all reasonable precautions to ensure that food is not exposed to risk of contamination either by their behaviour or lack of cleanliness
- ensure that good order and tidy conditions are maintained and that extraneous items, unconnected with the food business, are not allowed to accumulate in the preparation area
- keep the amount of food in storage to a workable minimum, ensuring that quantity and need are kept in balance
- identify and eliminate all entry routes and harbourage area for pests and attend to any relevant structural deficiencies
- rectify any damage or disrepair to the structure of the unit, facilities or equipment associated with the safe handling of food
- ensure that gas and electrical systems are safe and in good working order, and regularly checked by a competent person.

The following questions need to be asked:
- How does the event organiser ensure that they have both the best and the safest caterers?
- What precautions should the organiser take when employing caterers?

Again, 'Due Diligence' applies to both caterers and event organisers. The consequences can be serious if such diligence is not properly applied.

It has not yet sunk in with many organisers that the concession fee could be the least of an organiser's worries if things go wrong. Following a recent settlement of £1million for a pregnant mother who contracted salmonella from a salad, organisers need to take a serious look at what they are doing and why. It is not simply a matter of checking the caterer's insurance policy. If the caterer is not acting within the law, it is possible that the insurer could legitimately 'walk away' from any claim. That would leave both the organiser and the landowner fairly and squarely responsible as it is unlikely that, without insurance, the caterer would be able to meet a substantial claim.

The answer is that the organiser needs to carry out his/her part of the 'Due Diligence' trail by checking more than the caterer's insurance certificate. This need not be a burdensome task as most items that need checking can be done at the time of tendering or contracting the caterer. It is suggested that organisers should ask questions – and get copies of relevant documents – such as:

- Is at least one member of staff per unit trained to Basic Food Hygiene Level?
- Do you operate a due diligence system? If so, which one?
- Include a copy of your last gas compliance certificate/electrical compliance certificate.
- What source of power do you use?
- If you use petrol, what size petrol tank do you have?
- How much LPG do you carry?
- What refrigeration and freezing capability is there on your mobile(s)?
- Are your staff uniformed? Do they wear hats?
- What back-up storage facilities do you have?

If these and other checks are carried out, the risk of disasters would be reduced and the likelihood of liability would be minimised. MOCA advises organisers to issue a written contract with conditions clearly spelt out rather than depending on verbal agreements which, when things go wrong, can end in angry exchanges and lost reputations.

It is advisable for any event organiser to check that any outside caterers they use are members of MOCA, so ensuring that best practice is implemented as outlined above. Thanks are due to MOCA for providing information of the section dealing with Outside Catering. See the back of this book for further details.

h) marquees and tents

Marquee and tent hirers have a duty to ensure that members of the public can have complete confidence in the safety of the marquees and tents erected. In turn, organisers need to ensure that their suppliers operate to a code of practice when supplying marquees and textile-covered frame structures.

In addition, ancillary equipment supplied for use with such structures such as flooring, lighting, furniture, interior linings and heating should also be erected and installed in accordance with an approved code of practice. Usually such structures are supplied on a short-term or temporary basis. Long-term hire (ie more than 28 days) or semi-permanent installations, may be subject to other codes or regulations outside the scope of a limited period of a code of practice.

The Made-Up Textiles Association (MUTA) represents users, processors and manufacturers of all kinds of industrial textiles and is active in promoting technical standards in the industry. MUTA has published a code of practice for fabric structures and organisers are advised to contact MUTA for advice when considering the erection of temporary marquees and associated services.

In a bid to achieve even higher standards of public safety, a national training qualification for marquee erectors has been established.

This is the first time that a formal training qualification for operatives in the marquee hire industry has been set up. The initiative has come from the MUTA which represents more than three quarters of the UK's marquee hire industry.

The setting up of the National Vocational Qualification (NVQ) training scheme follows discussion between MUTA, Government Departments, including the Department of Employment and the Health and Safety Executive.

It is estimated that around 5,000 workers are involved in the business of erecting and finishing marquees, hospitality villages and sports event marquees throughout the UK. Currently, there is no recognised training scheme that employers can take advantage of to ensure their workers have the necessary skills and experience in erecting marquees.

A training manual is being put together and the funding of the NVQ scheme is being discussed.

The authors are indebted to MUTA for contributing this information on Marquees and Tents. Their contact address and telephone number is included in the listings at the back of this book.

i) accreditation

For some major events accreditation will be essential for security and access control reasons. However, even at smaller events, some recognition method may be essential for entry control.

It has also been suggested that accreditation or authorisation identification may well be useful or sometimes essential for insurance purposes.

If agreed to be necessary, then the accreditation system should be properly and carefully employed. It needs careful thought and planning and requires all staff to be fully trained in the requirements and procedures.

It is advisable to devise a rigorous accreditation scheme only where it is genuinely necessary; it will take a lot of work to implement and this should only be undertaken where it is worthwhile and essential.

j) road closures

Event organisers need to consider not just those involved in their event but also everyone affected by it. Many events (of any size) will affect traffic flow and planning must be considered carefully with this in mind.

Detailed discussions with the police force and other relevant agencies, such as the fire service and community groups, will be essential to ensure everything is taken into account and all essential permissions are obtained. Failure to follow mandatory procedures is another step to disaster and can cause last minute panic and ultimately cancellation.

It is all too easy to see this as a minor straightforward matter but unless it is properly handled it can be problematic. Like so many items in event planning, it requires serious detailed thought and appropriate action.

Normally any significant traffic interruption (over thirty minutes) will require an application and a formal road closure. This is not something that can be left to chance or arranged at the last minute. It will usually take a minimum of eight weeks to arrange. Remember – check it out. Speak to the police and the local authority officials at the start of your planning stages.

k) policing

Event organisers should remember that probably their best friends are the local police, given that you behave appropriately and involve them from the beginning.

Police attitude is very positive and generally supportive. Get them involved and keep them informed so that they can do their job as successfully as possible.

For the police force and indeed any stewards helping them, the key must be that they are there to help, not just control. They have a key role in genuine customer care, not customer discipline.

The key word used throughout is *involvement*. Police should be represented on organising groups and be seen as an integral part of the planning and delivery of any event from beginning to end.

They will have specific rules (and good behaviour) to enforce during the event and that is healthy and necessary. Good relationships can help get the best mutual approach to the policing of any event.

Give the police as much notice as possible that your event is happening because they may charge you a lot more if you give them a very short lead-in time. On the other hand, you may have good working relationships with the local police force and can persuade them to either waive or reduce their charges.

> Good sense is the concierge of the mind: its business is not to let suspicious-looking ideas enter or leave
>
> Laurence Sterne

technical aspects

★★★★★

FALL OUT AREA

minimum distance
50M

approximately
30M

SAFETY AREA

WIND DIRECTION

minimum distance
25M (more if possible)

AUDIENCE

a) firework displays

If you are organising your first display, you will find these notes very valuable. If you have had experience of organising previous displays, please use them as a checklist.

Choosing a venue
Always choose your venue in daylight. Make sure that it is large enough to accommodate your firing area and the number of spectators expected. Ensure that you can achieve the minimum safety distances required. Bear in mind that the number of spectators tend to increase each year

Consider how you will deal with disabled spectators.

Ensure that the site has plenty of unobstructed access and exit points. You will need at least one vehicle access point for emergency vehicles.

Ensure that noise from the display will not cause distress or disturbance to nearby hospitals, rest homes, animal sanctuaries or farm animals.

It is a great advantage for the site to be well served by public transport, thereby reducing the need for car parking facilities.

To some extent the choice of venue will determine what kind of fireworks you buy. If your site is level (eg a sports field) you would be well advised to use a large number of aerial fireworks (so the spectators at the back can see). If your firing area is elevated, ground level fireworks can be used to good effect.

The firing site
Remember that the spectators should be placed with their backs to the prevailing wind so that any smoke or debris blows away from the crowd. Be prepared for a sudden change of wind direction and have a reserve firing area available.

The firing area needs to be at least 60 metres wide and 30 metres deep with a fall out area at the back of at least 50 metres deep, preferably 100 metres plus.

The area should be away from overhanging trees or over-head wires and cleared of any combustible materials, including long grass and undergrowth.

The area should be securely fenced off before setting up the display, ideally with interlocking crowd barriers or chestnut paling. If you use rope and pin, use two lines of rope or tape, one at the top and another half way down.

Spectators should view from the front of the display only and not from the sides or back.

Who should be informed
The police need to know of any large gathering of people and any possible traffic congestion.

The fire brigade and ambulance service. They need to be notified of the display and the emergency vehicle access point to the site.

The local authority. Discuss your display with the local authority enforcement officer who will advise you on your duties under the Health and Safety at Work Act as well as noise nuisance. It is also worth checking whether they know of any other displays on the same night which may compete with your own.

The coastguard. If the site is near the sea, this will avoid possible confusion with distress flares.

The airport. Inform air traffic control if the site is near an airport.

Hospitals, old people's homes, animal sanctuaries and farmers. All should be notified.

Give everyone the VENUE, DATE and TIME.

IT IS STRONGLY RECOMMENDED THAT YOU HOLD AT LEAST ONE MEETING ON SITE WITH THE POLICE, LOCAL AUTHORITY, FIRE BRIGADE, FIRST AID SERVICE AND AMBULANCE SERVICE.

If you are organising a small, private display, you should still notify the police and anyone who may be disturbed by the noise.

Staffing
Stewards
Provide as many as you can and ensure that they are easily identified. Fluorescent waistcoats are ideal. The recommended minimum number of stewards is two for the first fifty spectators and one for each additional 250. Brief the stewards before-hand on the site layout, the plans for the evening and how to evacuate the site in the event of an emergency.

First aid services
Should be invited to attend and be on duty half an hour before the crowds arrive and remain until the site is clear.

Firing team
This is covered in more detail under 'Firing Procedures' below but as a general rule the number of personnel should be kept to a minimum.

Crowd control
Entrances and exits
Ensure that there are sufficient number of entrances and exits for spectators to be admitted in an orderly manner. Do not allow spectators to bring their own fireworks onto the site. Publicise that fact well in advance.

Public address
For larger displays a public address system should be provided. Hand-held loud hailers are very useful for smaller displays.

Bonfires
If you are having a bonfire ensure that it is well away and downwind from the firing area. It should be fenced off and supervised before, throughout and after the display. Do not use flammable liquids to light the bonfire and exclude anything hazardous from the bonfire material, eg aerosols, tins of paint, bottles, etc. If there is any risk of hot debris from the bonfire landing in the firework area DO NOT LIGHT THE BONFIRE. Make sure that the bonfire is **completely extinguished** before leaving the site.

Firing procedures
The number of operators should be kept to a minimum and preferably should have some experience. Each operator should have a particular firing job allocated and should familiarise him or herself beforehand.

Study the firing instructions and fireworks well in advance, preferably a day or two before the display.

All fireworks with aerial effects should be angled away from spectators so debris falls where it cannot cause injury or damage.

NEVER ANGLE FIREWORKS OVER THE HEADS OF SPECTATORS

Portfires

These are specially designed for lighting fireworks and are supplied. Only use portfires to light your fireworks. Do not carry portfires in your pockets. Leave them in a convenient place on the firing site in a closed box.

Equipment on the Firing Site

Fire fighting

An adequate number of fire extinguishers and supplies of sand and water should be provided. Certain stewards should be trained in the operation of fire fighting equipment as advised by the local fire brigade.

First aid

Have on the firing site a first aid kit. Include in the kit a roll of kitchen cling film and clean water. Clean any wound with water and wrap in cling film (excluding any parts of the face). Cling film is sterile, does not stick to wounds and protects burns, cuts and grazes until medical treatment is available.

Personal equipment for operators

Make sure that every operator is equipped with the following:
- overalls - cotton, preferably non-flammable (never use nylon)
- safety helmet
- eye and ear protection
- gloves
- torch
- hammer and nails
- scissors
- pliers
- baling wire or strong hemp cord
- matches

We strongly recommend that you use this information in conjunction with the HSE Guide Book - *Giving Your Own Firework Safety Display: How to Run and Fire It Safely*. (Ref/No.HS (G)124) available from good booksellers.

Firework safety and training

Pains Fireworks offer a comprehensive training course at their head office in Wiltshire and at their office in Newcastle.

The half-day course is run by Pains' in-house training teams and covers the setting-up and firing of a display, safety issues, crowd control and a host of other useful tips for a trouble-free evening. It is also a great opportunity to discuss your particular concerns with an expert.

Since the courses were introduced over ten years ago, community groups, schools, charities and numerous other organisations have all benefited from the professional expertise and advice of Pains Fireworks. As a result, hundreds of displays are now safer and more successful.

The authors are grateful to Pains Fireworks for this section on firework displays. See back of book for address.

b) ticketing

Admission by 'ticket only' is the ideal way of effectively managing the number of people attending an event but a decision about pricing levels is always difficult.

If an event is being staged for the first time, with no history of past success or failure, organisers may need to charge low ticket prices in order to buy customer loyalty for next time. Pricing also depends on the target audience and whether there are other competing events in the same area.

If tickets are to be sold, the box-office service is key to encouraging customers to attend year on year. Make it easy for people to buy tickets. The sales effort at the box office (or lack of it) can make or break the relationship with the organiser's potential audience.

For example, if organisers install a telephone hotline booking service, make sure calls are answered promptly and that the answering service is available at the publicised times. Make sure the customer is charged the correct amount, particularly if a concessionary ticket regime or differing pricing levels are in operation.

Also make sure that everyone is always clear, staff and customers alike, about who is entitled to receive concessionary rates. Publicise the policy for unsold tickets. Can people turn up on the day and buy a ticket? Will tickets NOT be available on the day? Are there stand-by arrangements?

Kalamazoo Security Print Limited issue a warning about ticket forgeries: "Whilst the actual cost of ticket fraud is uncertain – partly due to a lack of knowledge of how many tickets are forged and also due to an unwillingness by organisations faced with fraud to reveal the costs – fraud is increasing in the UK. According to the Metropolitan Fraud Office, the losses associated with paper-based fraud account for more than all burglaries, robberies and shoplifting put together."

"The leisure industry in particular is constantly at risk from fraud. By forging tickets for concerts, theatres and events, criminals can guarantee a rather attractive income at the expense of the organisers, the promoters, the artists and the public.

"Tickets are particularly susceptible to fraud because of both their high face value and because of limited supply. Unfortunately, as the technology behind colour photocopying, computers and desk top printing advances, fraud becomes easier and the risk to organisations becomes greater.

"However, many organisations, both large and small, may not realise the consequences of fraud. Not only does it result in lost revenue - for the organiser, the promoter and the artist - but can also be a serious safety risk.

"Take a music concert for instance. Whether staged in a huge concert hall or small club, if tickets are copied and pass off for sale as being originals , the venue loses out on sales to potential customers. This could be simply a few pounds for a small local theatre or music event or thousands of pounds for huge, high profile, pop concerts. Whatever the specific amount, its usually significant enough for any organisation to feel the losses.

"More importantly, by counterfeiting tickets and issuing them for sale, there are more tickets available than planned by the organisation and possibly more than the venue can legally accommodate, raising a health and safety issue.

"All entertainment venues have a limit to the number of people they can accommodate (whether seated or standing) under the Local Government Miscellaneous Provisions Act. These numbers are calculated by the fire authority in conjunction with the police prior to issuing a venue with an entertainments licence. Should that number be exceeded, the organisation will be in breach of the conditions of licence and the result can be a fine, loss of licence or

imprisonment. In addition, should anyone from the public be hurt through the organisation's negligence, it would also be liable to prosecution under civil law. This, of course, is a worst-case scenario but one that could very easily befall any organisation that does not take care to secure its tickets against fraud.

"Many organisations may not be aware of the existence of security tickets or their benefits. Security tickets simply include special covert (disguised) and overt (obvious to the holder) features that enable the box office or ticket collectors to ensure they are authentic".

Examples of some security features include:
- unique watermarks
- ultraviolet dull papers
- instant verification paper (when the ticket is marked with an instant verification pen, it turns pink)
- copy void background (if tickets are colour photocopied, the word 'VOID' becomes visible on the forgery)
- microtext (tiny printed codes which can only be read using a magnifying glass)
- solvent-sensitive paper (ensures no alterations can be made to the ticket through the use of solvents)

Tickets can be specially designed for the customer and incorporate any number of security features or the customer can choose to overprint customised information onto standard security tickets.

Remember that the licensing authority will require an audited account of the number of tickets sold. It is essential that tickets are numbered in order to lay the audit trail. Collection of tickets at the entrance to a venue is also very important and will help to avoid illegal entry.

The following is a list of tactics you may wish to implement when selling tickets for your event:
- provide a ticket hotline
- all return slips on brochures should be tagged in order to identify the most effective sales methods
- any advertisements in newspapers must carry a ticket booking slip (tagged) and should also carry a hotline number with a credit card booking facility, and also a method of payment through Giro (post office)
- publicity material must state who is eligible for concessionary tickets
- sell tickets at outlets other than the theatre, eg civic centre, library and other most frequented places in the area

- brochures should list stockists and sales points
- notices can be placed in Post Offices advertising discounted ticket rates for senior citizens
- brochures should contain information about catering facilities, content of the events programmes and venue access times
- contact social secretaries of groups/clubs offering party bookings (warning: group discounts may need to be restricted to certain performances)
- provide an 'easy to book' system
- install a booking offices at the venue or on site to be open during the week prior to the event and to be open every day
- brief box office staff to 'close sales' (ie persuade the uncertain customer that they should buy a ticket)
- use an advertising feature, eg 'ticket prices remain the same as last year'
- offer multiple attendance discount or season tickets
- if the event is a festival, set up a subscription scheme for 'Friends of the Festival' to encourage audiences to commit to purchasing tickets early
- insert brochures in newspapers
- try money-off coupons/gift vouchers
- 'standby' tickets could be heavily discounted and made available just hours before the event to attract marginal customers; advertise this only a couple of days prior to the event
- consider selling 'preview' tickets to show/concert rehearsals at discounted rates to lower income groups
- consider providing free car parking – if this is possible, use it as a promotional feature
- research rail travel/show packages if trying to attract audiences outside the area
- consider whether the event should coincide with or avoid school holidays

Kalamazoo Security Print Limited have contributed the technical information to this section on Ticketing and their advice is very much appreciated by the authors. You can find their address in the listings at the back of this book.

c) video production

As an organiser, have you ever considered making a video of your event, either to sell or for publicity purposes? Video is used by a growing number of organisations to boost their public profile or assist with staff communications, training and inductions.

However, taking your idea from script to screen, whether you are a big business, grassroots group or charity, needs careful consideration. There are key areas to which you need to pay close attention.

The most important thing has to be: know your audience.

Why do you want to commission a video in the first place? What are the expectations of the organisation you represent? Who will the video be aimed at and what do you hope your audience will get out of it?

It is no use making a video if it is going to sit on the shelf. You will also need to think about how it will be shown. Sometimes personal copies are sent through the post, allowing individuals to view the programme in the comfort of their own home and in their own time.

Perhaps you want to commission a video for use at a special presentation such as an annual meeting. Or maybe you want your video to be screened on a regular basis to groups of staff to assist with inductions or development.

It is worth thinking about a secondary audience. You might want your video to work harder for you and also double up as a device to explain the role of your organisation at meetings, when trying to attract public support or sponsorship.

Think long and hard about the message you want to get across and keep it simple and accessible. Trying to squeeze in too much information usually leads to confusion. Stick to the point.

Once you are clear about the sort of message you want to get across, you need to look at the on-screen presentation style. A professional production company will help guide you here but below are a few examples of how you can get your message across. Your choice will not just depend on your audience. Do not forget that there are likely to be budget implications.

Videos are usually recorded on Betacam SP, the current world standard broadcast format. You can create a mini documentary featuring a variety of interviewees and locations, linked together with a specially scripted voice-over. You will normally be able to keep a close eye on research and script development, working with the television production company you appoint to create a cohesive production. Regarding interviewees, do be brutal about whom you put in front of the camera. Television production companies will always work hard to get the best out of even the worst interviewee (it is in their interest as much as yours) but bear in mind that the obvious choice may not be the best. Be professional. Who do you think is 'televisual' and truly represents the ethos of your organisation?

Filming on location is considerably cheaper than hiring a studio and can lend your video presentation a sense of gritty – or glossy – reality. The right locations help build up a sense of pace and, combined with lively, enthusiastic interviews, keep the viewers watching.

Be inventive. More and more corporate video presentations feature dramatisations which can be a cost-effective way of getting your message across and might be worth considering as an alternative approach.

Re-creating events with actors, when imaginatively directed, is a powerful story-telling technique which never fails to engage the viewer; just look at the popularity of programmes like Crimewatch and 999. This can be especially useful if the message you are trying to get across is sensitive.

You can also make a powerful impression by simply combining a range of images, rather like a pop video, and adding a music backtrack; there need not be words and interviews at all. Often no more than two minutes long, this type of presentation can be particularly useful at public presentations and stands. Strong images draw the viewer in and it could be easily edited as a continuous loop.

These are just a few key approaches you might want to consider, depending on your budget.

In addition to filming interviews and gathering pictures there is a presenter and post-production (the trickery which create the final on-screen product) to consider.

What about graphics? The use and design of two-dimentional computer graphics and captions can help illustrate difficult, potentially confusing points such as facts, figures and procedures, and cosmetically contribute to the overall slickness of the presentation.

Have you thought about a presenter? A well-known celebrity will come at a price but they can lend your video kudos. You might prefer to consider voice-over artists. They usually charge by the hour and will link the various strands of your video

together in a less intrusive and anonymous fashion. Again, the production company you hire will assist you and help find the right voice, whether bright or authoritative, youthful or mature.

You may want to have your video adapted for other languages. This is easily achieved.

A few words about music: well chosen, it can assist the pace of the production and its overall quality. There are lots of technical options to consider which will have implications for your budget. Do not forget that music needs copyright clearance which can be costly (see section on PPL and PRS). Some organisations have their music written exclusively for them.

The tapes which create your video are called 'rushes' and will ultimately find their way into an edit suite. The cost of a production would include the services of an experienced broadcast picture editor to off-line edit your video, before the final compilation on-line.

Going through the rushes to find the best interview segments or sound bites and mixing them together can be a slow procedure but the attention to detail will pay off.

The number of filming days you require, the cost of travel, meals and accommodation for the crew, will have to come out of your budget.

Corporate television is not cheap but it is cost-effective. It can still be produced more quickly than a publicity brochure and is flexible and easily updated.

The best way to find a production company is by picking up the phone: ring around your friends, colleagues and contacts and ask them if they have any ideas.

Developing a relationship with the company which makes your video is important. There needs to be a sense of trust and mutual understanding.

If you would like more information about video production, look in the back of this book under Helpful Organisations to find information about Two Four Productions, a video production company which has a wide range of clients, including charities, government departments, industry and retail companies.

> Resolve to perform what you ought.
> Perform without fail what you resolve.
>
> Benjamin Franklin

chapter twelve

special events checklists and information

These checklists are compiled on the assumption that the basic programming for your event has been undertaken. They are designed to help you implement your plans.

a) conferences/seminars

- Create a critical path with timeframe.

- Prepare budget. Always make sure that you calculate the number of delegates you require in order for the event to break even. Keep budgets up to date and revised on a weekly basis.

- Book venue
  - Special room layout: theatre style, horseshoe, herringbone, classroom, etc
  - Ascertain whether there is a PA system
  - Check blackout facilities
  - Order refreshments and provide catering numbers (cater for people with special dietary requirements
  - Check disabled facilities
  - Ascertain price and whether this includes VAT
  - Ask for platform in main room
  - Check ceilings heights to ensure that screen is accurate size
  - Identify breakout rooms
  - Set up registration desk
  - Request a floorplan
  - Request a map/travel instructions
  - Request information on car parking
  - Information about accessibility, ie railways stations, taxis, etc
  - Check soundproofing
  - Is there any audiovisual equipment available and if so, is this included in price?
  - Check heating/air conditioning is not noisy
  - Reserve tables at lunchtime for speakers/VIPs

  - Prepare detailed operations timetable for organising staff and venue
  - Cloakroom to be available; is it free of charge?
  - Confirm access times

- Contact speakers
  - Brief speakers on date, time, place and conference theme
  - Confirm audiovisual requirements with speaker (overhead projector, slides, video, PowerPoint)
  - Provide visual aids preparation guidelines
  - Confirm overnight accommodation
  - Arrange rehearsal room for slides, etc
  - Send travel instructions, car parking arrangements, location of railway station, copy of final programme
  - Notify speakers about check-in/check-out arrangements at hotel
  - Notify speakers about travel/expense claims
  - Ask for highlights of presentation for publicity purposes
  - Request estimated time of arrival/departure
  - Tell speakers name of room to be used and number of delegates attending
  - Provide information about chair of the session and provide telephone contact number
  - Ask for copies of presentations in advance

- Appoint audiovisual company to provide:
  - Audiovisual equipment (see below)
  - Stage set (see below)
  - Lecterns
  - Logos for stage set
  - Speakers' table
  - Microphones

- Identify chair and provide
  - Briefing notes
  - Speakers' biographies to aid introduction

- Domestic announcements
- Emergency evacuation procedures to be read at the start of the day

- General
  - Provide delegate information pack
  - Delegate name badge
  - Delegate list
  - Provide a copy of final programme
  - Devise conference delegate evaluation sheet
  - Prepare lunch tickets, invitations, etc
  - Produce signs
  - Produce 'reserved' signs/speakers' nameplates
  - Hold on-site meeting with venue contact immediately prior to conference
  - Final briefing with chair immediately prior to conference
  - Ensure refreshment breaks provide soft drinks and water as well as tea and coffee
  - Invoice delegates and send acknowledgement letter, travel instructions, venue information

- Before you go
  - Compile a conference/seminar list before leaving the office: do not rely on your memory
  - Prepare a delegate questionnaire for issuing at end of event
  - Leave a copy of the following at the office:
    - telephone number of where you are staying
    - telephone number of the conference/seminar venue
    - map/travel instructions
    - delegate list

- On site
  - Set-up registration desk
  - Erect signs
  - Position speaker namecards on top table
  - Count chairs
  - Check number of chairs at speakers' table
  - Check all audiovisuals
  - Check that you know where light switches are situated
  - Check blackout arrangements are satisfactory
  - Ensure venue contact has your programme timings
  - Checkout location of cloakroom, toilets, public telephones
  - Make sure you have local taxi telephone numbers, how to get to nearest railway station
  - Fire alarm system
  - Location of fire exits
  - Disabled access: lifts, toilets, catering area, number of steps if no disabled lifts, availability of ramps, availability

of staff to assist
- Fifteen minutes before each break check catering arrangements
- During breaks ensure that venue has replenished water/glasses etc on top table
- Change speakers' nameplates if necessary

- Wind-up
  - Thank you letters to all involved
  - Invoice completed
  - Evaluate questionnaires
  - Replenish stationery box for next time

- Staff debriefing
  - What went well?
  - What can be improved?
  - How did staff perform? Invite self-assessment

- Audiovisual provision

Most audiovisual production companies will visit the venue with the client in advance of the event to ascertain the exact requirements. This is a valuable time because you will always find some extra needs to be addressed. It is worth noting which floor the presentation room is on and if there are any tight corners in which to move large pieces of equipment.

Once in the room, identify the full blackout facilities, whether they work, where the house lights are controlled from and, most importantly, whether there are any obstructions on the ceiling that can block the screen. One of the most common problems with older venues is chandeliers. They look wonderful but if they are situated so that they cast a shadow onto the screen find out whether they can be raised or removed. This can be a costly problem to solve and should be addressed at the earliest possible stage. Your event will only be successful if the audience can see the visuals and hear the sound!

When considering the screen size, the ceiling height must be taken into consideration. If you are using slides, you may need to have a square screen to accommodate landscape or portrait slides. As a rule of thumb the bottom of the screen should be at least 1.2m off the floor. This will allow people at the back of the room to see the whole screen without trying to peer around the heads of others. Always try to use the biggest screen possible. For example, for a room that is 18m long, a screen size of 2.4m wide is a minimum. The larger the room, the larger the screen needs to be.

If the room is large enough, you should consider using back projection. You will need 1.5 times the screen width behind the set plus 1m for the equipment. The advantages of back projection are that you get a clearer image and you can have more ambient light for the audience/delegates. Sound systems are also important. Never underestimate the number of loudspeakers required. It is much better to have an even level of sound through four speakers than blasting the front row of the audience and hoping that the people at the back of the room can also hear.

Proper microphone usage is important. No sound engineer can get clear amplification unless the presenters talk towards the microphones. Also consider the use of tie-clip microphones. These should not be obstructed by clothing and should be placed about 6 inches under the chin.

Question and answer microphones may be required for a larger auditorium and it is best if these are radio mics so that they can be easily passed to the person asking the question. Again, it is important that the delegate speaks into the microphone and does not gesticulate with it.

Preparation of slides and PowerPoint images must also be taken into account. Always use light text out of a dark background. This will make for a much clearer image when projected. With PowerPoint many presenters construct their own images and the presentation may look acceptable on a monitor on your desk but may not work when projected onto a large screen. For both slides and PowerPoint always use the largest typeface possible and do not place too much text on one image. Also do not take the text right to the edge as this may not project onto the screen.

Data projection is rapidly overtaking slide projection as the most popular medium for presentations. This presents its own challenges as does any ever-changing technology. Like computers, data projects seem to have a new and better model every three months. The brightness of data projectors is very important. This is measured in ANSI lumens and is a good and accurate guide to image brightness.

For a conference that uses a standard slide projector, a data projector should have a minimum of 450 ANSI lumens. Most new data projects exceed this brightness and as such, it is always advisable to get the brightest projector your budget can afford. Modern data projectors have the ability to interface with computers very quickly and are termed 'plug and play'. This means that if a presenter uses a lap top or Mac is can be connected directly to the data projector and the image will appear on the screen.

Should you have presenters wishing to use computer presentations, it would be advisable to have a dedicated computer for the purpose. The presenters then only need to bring a disk of the images and the technician can install them onto the show computer. Points to note are that the computer must run the latest version of PowerPoint and if your presenters put the information onto the disk, they must have the programme to de-compress the information, as there are so many versions available.

All data projectors will also project video images, provided you have a video player. VHS is still one of the most common formats but does not have the resolution and clarity of Betacam SP. Betacam tapes are of a broadcast quality and will provide an excellent image over a large screen.

If you are organising an international event, be very careful about video tape formats. Video tapes from America will be recorded using a system called NTSC and from France using SECAM and the UK system is PAL. Professional VHS players are triple standard, and this means that you can play video tapes from any format. However, it is always safer to check with your audiovisual company to make sure of compatibility.

• Stage sets
Stage sets will always enhance an event and will provide a central focal point for the audience. Stage sets come in many shapes and sizes with the main limitation for creativity being budget. For the smaller event you can use simple 'off the shelf' sets and screen surrounds. This cheaper option can be made to look exceptionally good with the addition of theatre lighting.

For the larger event, it is worth considering a custom-built set. This can be designed around the conference literature and programmes, reflecting the image for the event. Using this option you install a corporate identity and the overall effect is to portray a very professional image to your presenters and audience/delegates.

For larger conferences it may prove difficult for the audience to see the presenter at the lectern. To help with this problem many larger conferences use video relay. This involves the use of video cameras to relay the presenter onto a screen and provides all members of the audience with a good view.

Your technicians are the key to successful presentations and as such it helps if you and the technicians can build a rapport. If you have repeat events and wish to use the same audiovisual contractor, it is useful to request the same technicians who worked on your previous events. This will greatly reduce the amount of stress for the organiser as each party is familiar with each other's method of working.

You may wish to record the event for distribution at a later date. This could be either on audio tape or video. You can also use this to generate extra income at the event by selling on to the audience/delegates as a memento of the event or a valuable reference tool.

Finally, always give your audiovisual production company as much lead time as possible so that all the equipment and crew can be booked well in advance and remember that your AV production company will need to have access at least one day prior to the event.

AVT Limited is ILAM's preferred audiovisual and stage set contractors and the authors are grateful for their advice provided above. You can find their address and contact details listed at the back of this book

b) street parades

- Ensure you have local community awareness/involvement.
- Have a theme for the parade.
- Stage a competition for the best float. Number each float.
- Judge the competition in the 'holding area' before the parade commences.
- Set up a prize table in this area.
- It is easier to attract a sponsor if you have commercial vehicles within the parade.
- Link with a charity.
- Apply for a Street Collection Permit from the local authority. Try to provide twelve months notice.
- If you or the charity is collecting cash, what happens to the buckets of money en route?
- Apply for a Public Entertainments Licence if you intend to include music and dancing.
- Plan the route (avoiding passing the entrance of the ambulance or fire stations!).
- You may need to hire crash barriers.
- Consider whether portable toilets will be required.
- Try to ascertain from the local authority whether there

are any road works due to commence immediately prior to or on the parade date.
- Contact local utilities companies to ensure they have no road digging operations on the parade dates.
- Compile a signage schedule.
- Is the parade insured?
- Estimate assembly and dispersal times, and the duration of the actual parade.
- Notify police of road closure requirements.
- Seek police advice on car parking, 'holding areas' for all transport participating in the parade and those who are walking.
- Make sure a vet is on hand if animals are participating.
- Identify finishing place sufficiently large to hold the parade participants and spectators. Make sure that if there are gates to the area that they are sufficiently wide for parade lorries to enter and that there is a large enough turning area for the lorries.
- If the weather has been wet for a period before the parade, ensure that there is a supply of trakway to avoid lorries and other vehicles getting stuck in the mud.
- Consider whether you will be including music in the parade and if so, who will provide and how many 'sets' of music will be acceptable/entertaining?
- Employ ambulance services.
- Link with the aviation authorities to stage a parade 'flypast'
- Do you require civic involvement?
- Make VIP arrangements for sponsors/local dignitaries.
- Do you need to build a viewing platform?
- Will you require street entertainers to perform alongside the parade?
- Will there be street traders/food sellers along the parade route?
- Allow approximately one mile per hour as the parade travelling time.
- Notify public transport companies, including taxis, that their timetables may be slightly disrupted on the day of the parade.
- Notify the following local authority departments: leisure, planning, licensing, environmental health, direct services, mayor's office.
- Contact local press, radio, TV.
- Employ the services of stewards for crowd management, to walk at the side of the parade and in the assembly and arrival areas.
- Consider what you want to happen in the area where the parade arrives – a horse show? A family fun day?
- Ensure that you have good two-way communications with stewards, other organisers, etc.

c) opening and closing ceremonies

You might want to consider employing a professional production company to organise your opening and closing ceremonies. Otherwise you need to consider:
- timings and sequences
- rehearsal arrangements
- costumes
- flags and accessories
- balloons and inflatables
- minor works and construction
- musical arrangement
- theme songs
- choice
- sound effects
- sound track reproduction
- special effects
- choreography
- artistic, creative and lighting
- personnel and training
- budget and expenditure
- professional production
- key players
- master of ceremonies
- VIPs
- participants

d) protocol and VIP accommodation

You might want to consider:
- arrival and welcome
- baggage
- handbook manual
- registration
- protocol office
- protocol staff
- venue protocol
- hospitality
- victory VIP ceremonies/presentations
- VIP roll
- royal visit
- receptions and functions
- hotel accommodation
- accreditation
- ticketing and seating
- gold passes and car parking
- transport
- lounges
- toilets
- information
- liaison
- accompanying personnel
- departure

e) swimming event

The following information can be incorporated into an event requirements form:

Name of organising group:
Contact name:
Address:
Telephone: business: home: fax no: e-mail:

Event title:
Date:

Times:
Entry to changing:
Warm up:
Gala starts:
Gala finishes:

Numbers anticipated:
Guests:
Officials:
Swimmers:
Spectators:
Special guests:

Reserved seats:
How many?
Poolside for presentation of trophies
Overlooking pool
Finish
Shallow end
Second pool

Music and PA requirements:
Nature and time required
Location of microphone

Catering:
Numbers
Type of catering
Meal

Guests
Officials
Competitors
Time(s) required
Anticipated costs

Additional rooms
State no
Use and time

Additional information
(special requirements for guests, sponsors, etc)

Poolside requirements:
Number of lanes
Starting blocks nos – deep end
Number of chairs
Timekeepers – deep
Turn judges – boom
Finish judges – deep
Competitors – shallow
Competitors – deep
False start ropes
Referee/starter chairs
Announcers table/chair/microphone
Trophy table
Backstroke flags
Recorders table/chairs
Computer table
Winner's podium
Additional information
(ie timing pads, advertising banners, etc)

Pool layout
Please indicate preferred layout using diagram. Send copy
of diagram to floor manager, pool supervisor, etc.

f) fun run

The definition of a fun run is that prizes are not given
according to finishing position. Thus everybody may be
given a medal, or a spot prize may be handed out, but the
winner is not given a trophy or prize.

In fact this definition has become blurred and many fun
runs elect to provide prizes of one kind or another. The
advice given below is therefore relevant to organisers of all
running events.

Firstly, it is essential to be clear of your event's objectives
before proceeding. Therefore, you must ask yourself 'what
is the event's primary objective?' For example, is it:
• To raise money for charity? If so, a short distance event
  in a local park may be appropriate.
• To raise awareness of your organisation? A high-profile
  event with good quality medals provided is essential.
• To promote your running club? An accurately measured
  route starting and finishing near your club facilities is ideal.
• To add a good quality, well organised run to support the
  local running scene?

The checklist provided below is intended to address all
possible issues but bear in mind it will be influenced by the
following:
• your objectives
• your financial resources
• your staffing resources
• the area where you live

It must be stressed that however you choose to answer the
above the runners' needs must always come first. The
course must be safe, be cleared with the appropriate
authorities and be adequately marshalled. You must have
adequate public liability insurance and there must be
sufficient first aid support. These are the basic responsibilities
of the fun run organiser. It is advisable to take advice from
local runners.

There are specialist suppliers for most of the services listed
below. Get advice from others before ordering and get
quotations in advance.

Advice – usually free and easily obtainable from your local
authority, running club or athletics associations. Make sure
you use it!

Athletic club levy – if the event has a BAF permit (see BAF
in 'Helpful Organisations' section in this book), you should
charge every unaffiliated runner (ie runners who are not
members of a BAF registered running club) a £1 levy which
is then payable to the BAF.

Banners – you should have start and finish banners and
may wish to have some others, eg name of event. Decide
what logos and wording you want on them.

Bibs – all the event officials should be clearly identified. You may want them to be specific to their jobs, eg marshal, event director, etc. Running clubs and local authorities often have supplies which they may loan out.

British Athletics Federation (BAF) Permit – a fun run on its own does not require a permit. However, acquiring a permit will provide the event with public liability cover (via BAF). To get a permit contact your local athletic association and ask for the permit secretary. To get a permit the course must have been measured by a recognised course measurer (if it is promoted as an exact distance, eg the kilometre) and you must have consulted the police and the local authority. Contact BAF (UK Athletics '98) on 0121 456 5098 to get the contact details of your local permit secretary and course measurer.

NB At the time of writing BAF is in administration and their affairs are being dealt with by UK Athletics '98. However, BAF still regulates road running and issue permits and so it is a BAF permit that is required and it will still provide public liability insurance.

Budget – draft this at the initial planning stages. Make sure you allow for all the essential services and do not be tempted to scrimp on them.

Car parking – ensure you have space for the number of cars you expect plus the marshals and the signs to make sure they arrive at the right place. Bear it in mind you may need parking for your number of runners divided by two (ie 250 spaces for 500 runners). Publicise public transport alternatives when available.

Catering – even small runs may have sandwiches and hot drinks for sale. Not only is this a useful service for the runners and spectators, it may also be a money-raising exercise bene-fiting a local charity. Remember to cater for vegetarians.

Commentary – a good commentator will enhance the atmosphere of the event and help keep everybody informed. Ensure they have all relevant information about the event and a list of the runners' names and numbers (in numerical order). An assistant to help the commentator spot runners' names is also useful.

Date – you should avoid a clash with any other relevant local and significant national events (eg FA Cup Finals). Check local holidays and half-terms as well. Ensure venue is avail-able when you want it.

Deadlines – these will depend to some extent on the nature and objectives of your event. For example, a major fun run aiming to attract large numbers must be planned almost a year in advance whereas a low-key club event can be left a bit later.

You should work back from the date of the event and write in the deadline dates when the tasks must be completed. Don't forget that in the real world there are usually delays and you must allow for these in your planning.

Distance – fun runs tend to be any distance up to four miles. Above this is not really suitable for the 'occasional' runner and would be attractive mainly to regular runners who may not be your main target market. For children it must be a lot shorter. Therefore, refer to your main objectives and select the most appropriate distance. Take advice from others, such as a running club. The BAF stipulate the maximum distance children should run. The distance may be determined to an extent by the venue location and the length of course available.

Drinks – these must be provided at the finish. Water is the preferred option. Sweeter drinks such as orange squash need to be diluted more than usual. Tea and coffee should be provided for spectators as well as being popular with the runners on a cold day. Public health requirements should always be kept in mind and bottled drinks will be the safest to provide. Ensure you have enough for two per runner. A drinks station on the course will be needed for runs longer than 5km. They should be placed every 5km in these cases. Do not forget the litter implications.

Entry fees – make this value for money even if all proceeds are going to charity.

Entry forms and posters – your promotional material should always contain the following information: name of event, date, start time, venue, entry fee, how you can enter, contact name, address and daytime telephone number and sponsors' logos. The entry form should allow you to receive the following information from the entrant: name, address, age, sex, athletic club number, contact telephone number – plus anything that's relevant to your event.

Entry processing – make this computerised if possible. You must allow for a last minute rush of entries. If you keep the database of entries you can use it to mailout entry forms for next year's event.

Equipment – make a list of all the items you will need; you will find you keep adding to it! For example, tape, lump hammer, fencing pins, airhorn, clipboards, pens, tape, stopwatches, cups, cable ties and so on.

First aid – essential you do not cut corners with this. As an absolute minimum you should have first aiders at the finish. Depending on communication and ease of access, there may be other points on the course where they should be sited. Take the advice of the organisation you use (eg St. John Ambulance, Red Cross, paramedics). Ask around for the best one locally as the quality and reputation of the voluntary organisations varies from area to area. Make sure you give them a suitable donation.

Information – it is usually helpful to mail out runners' information prior to the event to all pre-entries. It should answer the questions the runners would have, eg venue, facilities available, time they need to report by, car parking, route and venue map and so on, plus any information specific to the event. You may also want to include their number and a sponsor form.

Main site – you will need to identify/arrange the following: toilets (will cause complaints if not sufficient), car parking, PA system (to keep people entertained, informed and relay important messages), registration point, changing rooms/area, signage, prize presentation point, tables and chairs. Additional facilities, such as a baggage store and refreshments, may also be appropriate to your event. Draw a site plan. Have a wet weather alternative plan.

Marshals – there should be sufficient marshals to direct and assist runners. They should wear conspicuous tabards or bibs. Make sure they are well briefed (in advance) as to their duties and responsibilities, have any items of equipment (eg walkie-talkies) they need and are in position in plenty of time. They should not direct traffic – that is the role of the police. Avoid using children except for tasks such as handing out medals and drinks at the finish. Do not forget to thank them and, if budget allows, give them a T-shirt or equivalent.

Medals (and ribbons) – decide what you want to give and budget accordingly, for example, a specially designed medal and ribbon or buy an off-the-shelf one. Note that medals may require up to eight weeks from placement of order to delivery, so you may well have to estimate the quantity required.

Miscellaneous – do you want to arrange some extras such as an aerobic warm-up, bouncy castle, entertainment, etc?

Numbers – decide on your numbering system and order appropriate quantities and number sequences. If you have a main sponsor ensure their name (and/or logo) is printed on them. Check delivery times with the supplier. Ensure you have some spares and blanks. Do not forget to get safety pins as well: runners often turn up without them.

Officials – an event with a BAF permit can request a referee, a chief timekeeper, recorders and a starter. Remember they may be in high demand so early booking is essential if required. See BAF.

On the day – equipment – meet the suppliers on arrival to ensure they are sited correctly. Prepare all the items you require in plenty of time.

On the day – staff – your action plan should highlight the staffing required. As an absolute minimum you need people to take responsibility for the following areas:
• enquiries/registration desk
• the start
• the finish
• marshalling

The event organiser should not allocate him/herself with specific duties. They need to be immediately available in case of any problems or emergencies.

Post event – it is not all over once the runners are finished. You will need to write thank you letters, send out results, issue press releases, pay invoices and tidy up all equipment.

Prize presentations – try to do these on the day and as soon as possible after the finish. The longer the prize list the longer it will take to check the results prior to the presentation. It helps to have an assistant to help with the presentation. Decide if you want a VIP/sponsor to give out the prizes. Remember what was said in the introduction about the definition of a fun run, however.

Programme – these can be time consuming to do and are only necessary for large events (2000+ entrants). Some companies specialise at putting programmes together through advertising sales.

Promotion – distribute your entry forms as widely as possible, eg at running clubs, sports shops, other runs, schools, etc. Ensure you send information to relevant 'What's On' columns and event listings at the right time (remember they may have copy deadlines several months in advance of your run). Do not forget to issue press releases and invite the local media on the day. Take photographs which you can use afterwards for the local press and for promotion the following year.

Public address system – this is recommended to keep people informed, entertained and to pass on important messages. Have a pre-event site meeting with the supplier to ascertain your requirements and location.

Public liability insurance – essential. See BAF

Radio communications – you need to be able to communicate to your staff and around the course. Use either walkie-talkies or mobile phones but check reception beforehand. Communications groups such as Raynet could be used for course communication.

Registration – unless entries are accepted on the day (for fun runs only), registration points should only be provided for enquiries, safety pins, etc.

Results – if you are producing results (strictly speaking, not for fun runs) it is recommended to use a results service or at least someone who is experienced and reliable. Ensure they are sited where the runners can't interrupt them. Computerised systems are essential for all but the smallest runs. You may want to provide envelopes for runners to put their name and address on and leave with fifty pence for results to be sent to them.

Route – ideally it will be on closed roads or in a traffic-free area (this is a definite requirement for children's events). If you must use roads you must liaise with the police and the local authority. Go for an anti-clockwise course to minimise road crossings. You may decide to do laps but do not have more than three (less for shorter than a two mile run). A loop course is easier to manage than a point-to-point or out-and-back.

Rules – at the initial planning decide on the event rules and items such as age categories, team prizes (and number to count) and set out definitions, eg what is meant by a 'local runner'.

Runners with special needs – you will have entrants and spectators with special needs. These may vary from athletes using wheelchairs to blind runners. Ensure your route, facilitie (including toilets and signage) are as accessible as possible. If in doubt, seek advice from your local authority or a local sports club run by disabled people.

Signage – used for the route, around the main site and for finding the venue. Distance markers can also be used although take care if using a lap course that they are not confusing. Designs on a fluorescent background are the most effective.

Sponsors – as well as trying for cash, do not forget to look for help in kind. For example, a garage may supply a lead car. Remember to acknowledge this support and to write to them formally afterwards.

Start and finish – allow sufficient space and for ease of movement through. Have an event clock under the gantry if appropriate. Use banners to highlight them.

T-shirts – if you choose to have t-shirts make sure they are of a reasonable quality. It is counter-productive to provide shirts which fade or shrink in the first wash. This is a very competitive field so check out a number of suppliers and prices in advance.

Timekeeping – arrange timekeepers and number recorders, if necessary. They should work in pairs. Arrange recording equipment (watches, clipboards, waterproof covers, recording sheets, pencils). See BAF and officials.

Toilets – essential and do not forget there is a concentrated period just prior to the run when they are in big demand. Ensure you have plenty for the expected number of runners and spectators.

Trophies and prizes – if it is a fun run make sure that prizes are spread throughout the field.

Checklist:

Banners
- ☐ requirements and design
- ☐ order
- ☐ check delivery

Bibs
- ☐ quantity
- ☐ order
- ☐ check

Commentary
- ☐ book commentator
- ☐ location
- ☐ prepare commentary notes

Date
- ☐ check suitability and availability of venue
- ☐ decision and advertise

Drinks
- ☐ quantity
- ☐ order
- ☐ delivery arrangements

Entry form and poster
- ☐ produce first draft
- ☐ amendments
- ☐ final draft
- ☐ production

Entry processing
- ☐ procedure
- ☐ system setup
- ☐ checking

Equipment
- ☐ list
- ☐ arrange (purchase/borrow)

First aid
- ☐ requirements
- ☐ book Red Cross/St. John/paramedics

Format and procedures
- ☐ draft and circulate
- ☐ information
- ☐ compilation
- ☐ check drafts and amendments
- ☐ check with third party
- ☐ production

Insurance
- ☐ arrange sufficient cover

Main site
- ☐ toilets
- ☐ car parking
- ☐ public address
- ☐ registration point
- ☐ changing rooms
- ☐ signage
- ☐ presentation point
- ☐ tables
- ☐ site management and equipment

Marshals
- ☐ number
- ☐ recruitment
- ☐ allocation of duties:
  - • start
  - • course
  - • finish
  - • car park
  - • registration
  - • main site
- ☐ pre-event check
- ☐ issue of info packs

Medals (and ribbons)
- ☐ design
- ☐ order
- ☐ check delivery

Miscellaneous
- ☐ entertainers
  - • budget
  - • arrange
  - • ascertain their needs
- ☐ music
  - • arrange
- ☐ warm up – yes/no – if yes:
  - • book instructor
  - • confirm requirements and arrange

Numbers
- ☐ requirement and design
- ☐ order
- ☐ check delivery

On the day action plan
- ☐ production of plan
- ☐ distribution of plan

On the day – equipment
- ☐ prepare recording sheets
- ☐ prepare enquiries desk items
- ☐ prepare display boards
- ☐ prepare all equipment required
- ☐ arrange delivery and return

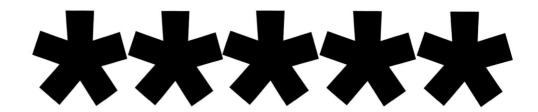

On the day – staff
- ☐ allocation of duties
- ☐ briefing

PA system
- ☐ requirement
- ☐ check if internal and external PA required – ensure covers all areas where people will be
- ☐ site meeting – location of caravan and speakers
- ☐ order

Post event
- ☐ production and distribution of certificates and results
- ☐ payment of invoices
- ☐ write event report – include all areas as in checklist
- ☐ thank you letters and payment of invoices

Presentation
- ☐ arrange VIPs
- ☐ decide on order

Programme
- ☐ decide if to do one. If yes:
  - adverts
  - copy
  - check draft
  - production

Promotion
- ☐ information into appropriate listings
- ☐ distribution of forms and posters
- ☐ media releases
- ☐ photocalls

Radio communications
- ☐ requirements
- ☐ book a communications group or arrange hire of walkie-talkies
- ☐ communication plan and locations
- ☐ signing out sheet for walkie-talkies (if hiring)

Results
- ☐ decision on whether needed
- ☐ if so, book results service
- ☐ check they are familiar with format and needs
- ☐ production of recording material and timesheets

Route
- ☐ police
- ☐ highways department
- ☐ notification to fire brigade and ambulance services
- ☐ course measurement
- ☐ lead bike
- ☐ sweep vehicle

Signage
- ☐ requirements
- ☐ order
- ☐ check delivery

Start and finish
- ☐ location
- ☐ gantry
- ☐ barriers
- ☐ map
- ☐ procedure
- ☐ canopy for recorders
- ☐ drinks and medals tables

Timekeeping
- ☐ arrange timekeepers and recorders if necessary
- ☐ arrange recording equipment (watches, clipboards, waterproof covers, recording sheets, pencils)

Toilets
- ☐ necessary? – if yes
  - ☐ quantity
  - ☐ order
  - ☐ location

Trophies and prizes
- ☐ requirements
- ☐ order
- ☐ check delivery

T-shirts
- ☐ quantity
- ☐ order
- ☐ check

Thanks are due to Health Start for contributing this checklist. Their address is at the back of this book.

g) outdoor concert

Source of reference – *Guide to Health, Safety and Welfare at Pop Concerts and Similar Events*

The site
- suitability.
- concert arena – capacity
- access and egress routes
- if the site grazed livestock will need to be removed
- car parking area – access and egress routes
- surrounding roads – potential bottle necks and dangerous black spots
- security
- safety – any hazards such as deep water, uneven ground etc

Entertainment license
- licence fee
- site plan
- technical information
- risk assessments and safety policies

Stage
- chairs
- music stands
- music
- lights

Fireworks
- safety distances to audience
- prevailing wind
- identification of hazards such as a dry crop, livestock, local residents or close proximity of firing site to surround buildings

Technical crew
- site manager
- electrician

Power
- Which areas need power? eg staging, toilets, marquees, etc.
- How many generators will be required?

Ticket checking
- location of ticket checkpoints – will it be carried out on foot or in cars?
- design of ticket checkpoint so as not to cause delays
- signage and lane demarcations
- numbers of staff

Programme
- float
- programme sellers

Stewards
- 1 steward per 250 audience
- fluorescent jackets
- chief steward
- clear and concise briefing of stewards to define their role on site
- identification of any hazards on site

On-site signage
- toilets
- first aid

- exits
- fire point

Toilets – see Chapter Ten re toilet provision

Car parking
- Distance between the car park and the concert site – how far?
- Condition of the ground? Will you need four-wheel drives to pull vehicles out in wet conditions?
- Will additional hard core be required at entrance and exit points?
- Designated area for disabled drivers.

Road signs

Lighting towers
- lighting of the route back to the car parks and the car park area
- lighting of any potential hazard area such as gateways

Fencing
- fencing of hazards, eg fireworks, steep slopes, trip hazards, deep water, etc
- backstage areas

Orchestra and artists changing facilities
- agent's booking arrangements
- on-site facilities for performers, eg refreshments and changing rooms

Litter clearance
- bins
- skips
- litter bags

First aid cover
- number of first aiders
- number of ambulances
- number of first aid posts
- will a paramedic crew be required?

Police cover
- are the police required on the road to aid the access and egress of cars?
- are the police required on the concert site for crowd safety reasons?

Fire brigade
- will the fire brigade be required to be in attendance?
- fire fighting equipment on site in all marquees, stage area, etc
- location of designated fire point

Communications
- mobile radios
- mobile phones
- key personnel

Tickets
- where will they be sold?
- security?

Publicity
- leaflets
- distribution
- tickets
- box offices

This checklist was contributed by Performing Arts Management which stages over thirty open air concerts every year. Their information can be found at the back of this book.

h) street entertainment

Street art is already the most popular and innovative art form in mainland Europe. Each year large-scale street arts festivals are produced across the continent presenting art of the highest quality from professional performers.

Street art is the most celebratory, accessible and all-embracing of art forms incorporating traditional and contemporary music and dance, circus, theatre, mime, visual art, carnival arts, pyrotechnics and new technologies.

The last ten years has seen a rapid increase in the quantity and quality of street arts and street art events in this country. This is an exciting time for the artform as we approach the new millennium and street arts comes into its own as the artform of the twenty-first century.

There are a number of fundamental issues which prospective producers should bear in mind when planning a street art event.

Programme
An imaginative and innovative approach should be taken to programming to avoid the cries of "Oh no, not another juggler!" at your event. Recent events have seen contemporary dance in wheelchairs in Bristol City Centre and flamenco on the streets of Lewisham. Both of these performances were great successes and there is something magical about presenting the unexpected in an everyday environment. Street art is also a great social ambassador. Work with local professional artists and community groups to develop performances unique to your locality.

As audiences become more educated there is more pressure on the producer to offer high quality. This can only be a good thing. You can lessen the risk of presenting inappropriate or poor performance by maintaining a policy of only programming shows that you have seen or by employing the services of a reputable specialist street arts producer or agency to programme the event for you. This is especially true in the case of presenting international work which tends to be more expensive and production intensive than UK work. It is never advisable to be tempted to sacrifice quality of performance for quantity. The public will be more likely to remember one amazing performance than five insignificant shows.

Artist availability can affect the quality of programme that you can present. The availability of the most successful artists becomes a problem in the busy summer season and the situation is unlikely to get any better.

Artists should be matched to the site and the prospective audience. Choose the site very carefully and consider factors such as artist's technical provision, shelter for the audience and the performers, audience sightlines, pedestrian and vehicle traffic routes, proximity to artist dressing rooms, acoustics and noise interference from nearby roads and businesses.

An artist's technical requirements should be considered before a programme is finalised as they will certainly have an important effect on the overall event budget. A basic technical provision can sometimes double the performer's fee.

Most artists will have a clear printed sheet detailing their technical requirements. This should include details such as:
- minimum size of performance space and any special site requirements, ie vehicle access, no balconies, whether the show is performed front-on or in the round and so on

- duration of show and the number of times it can be performed
- power requirements
- whether a PA is needed and who should supply it
- dressing room requirements
- parking requirements
- security provision: it may be that overnight security is required
- details of get-in and get-out times
- what accommodation and food should be provided by the producer

If an artist does not have a specific list of requirements it is advisable to go through each of these items with them and confirm them in writing. Technical provision details often form part of the producer/artist contract.

Liaison
Maintaining close liaison between all the disparate groups involved in a street arts event is absolutely crucial to the safe and successful production of an event. The producer's role is to ensure the reliability and clarity of all information and that it is communicated to all necessary parties prior to the event.

Artists
There should be a signed contract between the artists and the producer clearly stating the rights and duties of each party. This will prevent any misunderstandings in the event of a later incident. The artists should also be sent clear details well in advance of the event including a map indicating access, performance space, dressing rooms and allocated parking spaces; a performance schedule; confirmation of agreed technical provision; background details of the event including any print marketing; an agreed arrival time and the name and contact number of the producer's on-site representative.

If the performance is a large-scale show that may present production difficulties, eg if it contains pyrotechnics then a site visit between the producer, the artist and the relevant authorities (see below) should be arranged well in advance of the event. This is especially true for international companies and is well worth the extra expense. Happy artists equal a happy event.

Authorities
There are many different authorities that need to be considered in the pre-production of an event that will take place in a busy public place.

The authorities to contact will vary according to the size of the event but do consider the following:
- the local authority
- environmental health
- licensing
- leisure services department
- police
- fire services
- first aid
- town centre manager
- shopping centre management
- local traders' association
- local residents' association

If road closures are needed you should also work with the Traffic and Highways Department and be sure to notify bus and taxi operatives and any sections of the public who are likely to be affected.

The best way to inform all the relevant authorities is to produce and circulate an event manual as soon as the programme is finalised. This document should include background details about the event, details of the performance site/s, performance and production schedule, details of technical provision, information about the artists that will be performing, details of any road closures, contact details of the producers, risk assessments and ways in which the risks will be dealt with: provision of stewards, fire extinguishers, hand held radios, emergency evacuation procedures and crowd control and so on.

After the event manual has been circulated an initial round-table meeting should be arranged. This provides the authorities with the opportunity to ask any questions and make any additional suggestions. These recommendations should be incorporated into the revised event manual. Again this should be circulated and a final round-table meeting is arranged just prior to the event.

Finally, the practical information from this last meeting should be bound into an operational document for use by the event team and relevant authorities on the day. This includes performance and production schedule, site maps, contact details, event personnel information and radio procedures.

Health and safety

The health and safety of an event is of paramount importance. New legislation means that risk assessments will need to be produced for all public events and street arts producers are well advised to familiarise themselves with this procedure.

Aspects of risk management include the numbers of event stewards that will be needed, methods of communication between the event team and emergency services, safety distances, barrier provision, first aid cover, certification and inspections, fire precautions and so on.

Any temporary structures or power supplies should be inspected and signed off by qualified personnel. This is a stipulation of many local authority licensing procedures. Most free street arts events are not liable to a licensing fee but the event producer should still fulfil all the requirements of the licensing application.

If any pyrotechnics are to be used these should be cleared by the local fire officer. There should be an experienced and licensed pyrotechnician responsible for igniting the pyrotechnics and ensuring all safety regulations relating to the storage and use of pyrotechnics are adhered to.

Another note on health and safety: always stipulate that artists and clients carry their own public liability insurance as well as carrying a £5million public liability insurance. Any hired equipment should also be insured. Overlooking this could prove to be expensive.

Wet weather

The British audience is heartier than you may think when it comes to enjoying themselves. You should work out your wet weather policy as early as possible and incorporate this into the artist contract and the event manual.

Always remember that if an artist has turned up they want to perform and will do so unless it presents a serious risk to life or limb to continue.

One way to prevent a complete washout is to locate an alternative venue in the case of wet weather: an indoor shopping centre or community centre. If you do decide to do this ensure that you include this somewhere on your publicity and that resilient stewards remain in the original venue to direct the audience to the new performance site. A-boards are invaluable at a time like this.

Remember the following points:
- be careful in your choice of site
- stress quality and range of work in your programming.
- you have the opportunity to create a high-quality celebratory arts event that brings the whole community together
- always choose a programme that is suitable to the site and potential audience
- ensure you have an experienced, friendly event team and that they are briefed about the event so they can inform the public
- market and publicise the event fully and effectively
- ensure that you produce a clear and concise event maual and stick with it

This information was produced by Dave Reeves, Director at Zap Productions which has organised successful large- and small-scale outdoor events since 1989. In 1997 they were awarded a grant of £400,000 from the National Lottery through the Arts Council of England to produce the National Street Arts Festival. In all they produced over fifty events in parks, shopping centres, town centres, seafronts and village squares.

The the events are free to the public and are funded by a mixed economy of private and public monies. Their aim is to work with like-minded festival partners across the country to increase participation in and appreciation of UK street arts and to generate greater public, media and funder interest in street arts. You can find more information about Zap Productions at the back of this book.

i) administration checklist

These can vary from event to event but here are some of the areas that may be included:
- accommodation
- accreditation
- administration services
- application forms
- appeals
- arrivals/departures
- bills
- budgets
- cash
- checklists
- communications
- computers

- contracts
- copyright
- documentation
- franchise
- information storage and retrieval
- insurance
- invitations
- invoices
- legal considerations
- letters
- licensing
- organisation structure
- overall timetable
- public address support
- passes
- printing
- programmes
- research
- reporting systems
- sales
- schedules
- seating
- stationery
- stock checking
- tickets

j) volunteer checklist

- identification
- sources
- recruitment
- training
- management
- motivation
- reward
- recognition
- catering
- accreditation
- transport
- mementos
- role/responsibility

k) a master events checklist

- access times
- accessibility
- accommodation
- accounts
- accreditation
- acoustics
- administration
- admissions
- advertising
- agencies
- agents
- aims
- alcohol
- ancillary activities
- ancillary facilities
- announcements
- appeals for funds
- appeals for volunteers
- application forms
- arrival/departure times
- artistes
- artwork
- atmosphere
- audience
- audio visual requirements
- audit
- badges
- banking
- banners
- barriers
- big screen hire
- blackout facilities
- bookings
- box office
- budgeting procedures
- business plan
- Calor Gas
- cancellation
- car parking
- cash collection
- cash flow/change
- catering
- ceremonies
- certificates
- chairperson
- chairs and tables
- changing rooms

- charities
- checklists
- children
- children's act
- church services
- civic/government receptions
- cleaners
- cloakrooms
- colour theme
- commentators
- committees
- communications
- community
- competitors
- complaints procedures
- complimentary tickets
- computers
- concessions
- contingency plans
- contractors
- contracts
- copyright
- creche
- critical plan document
- crowd management and flow
- currency rates
- customer care
- date
- debriefing
- decoration
- delegates
- demonstrations
- departure arrangements
- dietary requirements
- diplomacy
- direct mailhosts/hostesses
- disabled facilities
- display boards
- displays
- documentation
- donations
- drainage
- drug testing
- duty of care
- electrical supply
- electricians
- electricity
- e-mail
- emergency procedures
- emergency services
- enquiries
- entertainment
- entrances
- entry arrangements
- equipment
- estimates – income/expenditure
- evaluation (post-event)
- event handbook
- exchange facilities
- exhibitions
- exhibits
- exits
- facilities at venue
- facsimile
- feasibility study
- fees
- fencing
- films
- financial planning policing
- fire regulations
- fireworks
- first aid
- flags
- float of small change
- floral decorations
- food hygiene backstage
- franchise arrangements
- fund raising
- gas
- general public
- gifts
- grant aid
- greeting and seating
- ground conditions
- guests
- Health and Safety Act
- hiring
- hospitality
- hosting
- hotels
- identification
- image
- income and expenditure
- information
- insurance
- internet
- interpreters
- interviews

- invitations
- invoicing
- lasers
- lecterns
- legal considerations
- letters
- liaison officers
- licenses
- lifeguards
- lighting
- litter collection
- loading/unloading facilities
- local authority
- location
- logos
- lost children
- lost property
- lotteries
- maintenance
- manpower
- maps
- market research
- marketing
- marquees
- master of ceremonies
- medals
- media
- medical provision
- meeting plans
- menus
- merchandising
- message board
- messages
- microphones
- mission statement
- mobile phones
- monitoring
- music requirements
- newspapers
- no-shows
- noise
- numbers participating
- objectives
- offices
- officials
- organisational plan
- participants
- partnerships
- passes

- patents
- patronage
- performers
- performing rights
- permits
- photocall
- photocopier
- photography
- pit areas
- planning
- plans
- policing
- political support
- post-event arrangements
- poster sites
- power supply
- practice facilities
- presentations
- press
- press conference
- press launch
- press releases
- press room
- prestigious supporters
- pricing policy
- printed programme
- printing
- prizes
- programme
- promotion
- protective clothing
- protocol
- public address system
- public consultation
- public liability
- public relations
- public transport
- publicity
- radio
- raffles
- receipt systems
- reception areas
- recycling
- refreshment breaks
- refunds
- refuse areas and disposal
- registration
- rehearsals
- religious services

- reporting systems
- research
- reservations
- resources
- results board
- retail outlets
- risk assessment
- safety
- sales
- schedules
- scoreboards
- seating
- seating arrangements
- secretarial services
- security
- services (electricity etc)
- shops
- signage
- signposting
- sound
- sound checks
- soundproofing
- souvenirs
- speakers
- spectators
- spectators' arrangements
- sponsors
- sponsorship
- staff/stewards
- staging
- stall holders
- stationery
- stewarding
- stock checking
- stockchecks
- storage
- strategies
- street entertainment
- structures (or organisation)
- subsistence
- Sunday Trading Law
- support services
- SWOT analysis
- tasks
- taxis/coaches
- team liaison
- technical equipment
- technical requirements
- technicians
- technology
- telephone
- telephone sales
- teletext
- television
- tents
- thank yous
- ticketing
- tickets
- timetable
- toilets
- tombola
- top table
- tourist services
- traders/exhibitors
- traffic control
- training
- transport
- travel (agents)
- trophies
- two-way radios
- uniform
- ushers
- Value Added Tax
- venue(s)
- VIPs
- visitor facilities
- visual scoring
- volunteers
- warm up
- waste disposal
- water supplies
- weather contingencies
- welfare
- wheelchair hire
- work schedules

The life so short, the craft so long to learn

Hippocrates

chapter thirteen

help, advice and support

Probably as many people get involved in event management by accident, through voluntary involvement or change of job, as those who conciously make career moves into this field.

This is due to the shortage of training available to support this experience and also to the feel of insecurity ("Have I done everything?") which constantly prevails in events. It is difficult to get a great deal of information even from people who have been heavily involved (hence this book). This is partly due to the fact that so many events have little written information that can be passed on and partly because many experiences are so individual.

It is sensible to remember that few projects are totally novel or unique. It is very likely that someone has previously done something at least similar to your venture. Identifying them and picking their brains is going to make your task much easier and probably more successful. It is always better to learn from the mistakes of others rather than your own.

Given time, most event organisers are only too happy to relate the details of their experiences. It is foolish not to take advantage of this source of wisdom.

The enthusiasm and camaraderie of event organisers is one of the the most supportive influences around. It will help keep others motivated even when they face an apparently insurmountable crisis. It is always nice to know that others have faced the same problems and probably have a solution that you can adopt.

Hopefully the information which follows will provide you with that much needed support.

a) groups of people who can help

- Local authority staff
- Emergency services – fire, police, ambulance
- Lawyers
- Accountants
- PR agencies
- National organisations (eg Arts Councils, Sports Councils)
- Insurance brokers
- Medical professionals
- Information technology specialists
- Environmental Health Officers
- Special service providers (eg firework companies, waste disposals firms, etc)
- Event organising agents (eg ILAM Services Limited)

b) information technology

As an event organiser you will need to ensure that you are ready to use information technology as required:
- Project management software
- Pagers
- Fax (facsimile)
- Word processing
- Video conferencing
- Audio conferencing
- Computer recording
- CD ROM
- Radios
- Interactive video disk
- Computerised result systems
- E-mail
- Computer conferencing
- Internet (and the world wide web)
- Mobile/car phone

If you have no idea how some of these media might benefit you, then you should find out. Speak to colleagues, organisers of other events and the suppliers of technology.

All of these developments and the facilities they bring to events can ease and enhance effective planning, communication and delivery.

They will make events easier to organise, so make the maximum use of them.

c) public consultation

A structured programme of public consultation is enormously beneficial to the development of a programme of festivals and events.

Public consultation will:
- identify the aspirations of the community
- identify the priorities of the community
- identify the input that the community wishes to make
- build on the expertise available in the community
- share information

It is essential that the consultation take place within a strategic framework and within set financial parameters. Unless this is done, public ideas and expectations may rise to a level that is beyond that which can be provided by the organiser.

A key component of consultation should be with local organisations, schools, traders organisations, community associations and organisations consulted on previous events.

Consideration should also be given to involving representatives of the community on a steering group. However, such organisations are likely to have vested interests and will, therefore, be in a difficult position when it comes to taking an overview. It is therefore suggested that community groups are not invited onto a steering group but that one of the roles of any steering group will be to ensure that a programme of public consultation is undertaken.

Mike Fulford, consultant with Leisure Advice, is an expert on public consultation and his details can be found in the back of this book.

d) alcohol – use/abuse

Organisers can often see alcohol as an integral part of their event and see its provision as a significant part of their income flow.

This may be so but it brings its own hazards, legislation and need for careful monitoring and control. Even in the corporate hospitality tent it can cause problems which can spill over into other aspects of the event.

Properly controlled, alcohol can be a major bonus and add a social dimension, as well as income, to a range of events.

Legislation is strict and any national or local regulations must be tightly followed. Failure to comply at any point can lead to instant closure and consequent problems.

Provision must also be made in planning to deal with any alcohol abuse, subsequent rowdiness or inappropriate behaviour. Clear plans must be compiled for stewarding and/or ejection or other appropriate action before the event commences; this avoids a potential crisis management situation.

If alcohol is worth providing, it is worth providing for its possible consequences.

e) drugs – use/abuse

Organisers will need to consider the possibility of drug use/abuse at their events. This is a matter for discussion with the police authorities. Ultimately their view and authority will have to be adhered to.

Ideally organisers should provide a 'refuge' for drug takers and counselling facilities for those suffering the ill-effects of drugs, with a reassurance that this will not necessarily be a road to criminal retribution. This scenario is particularly relevant to the rock and pop concert industry.

Legal action is the remit of the police who will decide any course of action to be taken. The organiser's role is to assist the police in identifying the problem.

f) tips for the event organiser

- As far as fetes and carnivals are concerned, advise your staff and concession holders to give out change to customers in coinage not bank notes. People will always spend the change in their pockets or purses but will not always be willing to break in to a bank note.

- Staff at events should always wear identification tags. These are required for safety and insurance purposes as well as for ease of identification.

- Recruit a team of litter pickers who will turn up at the end of your event, rather than use tired events staff.

- Always check the spelling on your posters. Your image will be in tatters if you make a spelling mistake on directional signs and posters.

- If you are providing changing areas for performers on a greenfield site, make sure you provide separate female/male facilities.

- Stallholders may be holding raffles or tombolas and will, in all probability, have bottles of alcohol as prizes. In order to ensure that people who are under the age of 18 do not have access to alcoholic prizes, ask the stallholder to deliver these prizes to the home of the winner and deliver into the safekeeping of an adult (note: raffle tickets should not in any case be sold to anyone under the age of 18).

- Do not allow events staff to consume alcohol either before or during an event.

- Remember that cars with catalytic converters should not be allowed to park on long grass. In dry weather, this is a fire risk.

- Tell the police well in advance about your event. Short notice can lead to higher policing charges.

- Don't use cannons/guns to start a street parade if the parade includes animals, especially horses.

- Good publicity is vital. No-one will come if they don't hear about it.

- Write everything down. The key organiser could get knocked down by a bus.

- Do not make presentations or closing ceremonies too long. They leave a bad impression even if the event has been good.

- Keep staff fully in the picture through regular brief update meetings.

- Put all agreements in writing.

- Keep a sense of humour: it is a vital ingredient.

- Check, check, check and check again.

- You have got to pay attention to detail.

- Always learn from the mistakes of others, not your own.

- Ask! There's usually someone who has been there before.

- Look after your customers and they will come back.

- Every event is different.

- Quality people are the key to quality events.

- If you can't do it well, think again!

- With hard work, a good team and good leadership, anything is possible.

- Resource management is key to event management.

- Do not reach for the sky if you have not got the resources.

- Volunteers are good for events if they are given good guidance.

- Event skills are transferable, eg sports to heritage or vice versa.

- It won't be alright on the night.

- A good team produces good events.

- The event participant is king!

- Always have a 'meeter' and 'greeter' on site to look after guests and VIPs on arrival.

- If a large amount of cash is expected on site, make suitable arrangements for its safe collection at regular intervals during the event, and for its stage storage and/or banking.

- Produce a printing schedule at the planning stages so as to secure your print slot at the printers.

- Make sure that everyone involved in the event knows who is in charge.

- Get a charity involved, preferably with a high-profile patron.

- Do not take chances: employ qualified stewards to take care of your audience.

- Have a contingency plan for cancellation/ postponement of your event.

- It is bad PR to have too few toilets. Make sure you have estimated realistically and do not cut costs.

- Remember to cater for a wide variety of dietary requirements.

- It is usually easier to find sponsorship 'in kind' than 'in cash'.

- Access, facilities, amenities and programmes must be considered to enable people with all types of disability to participate.

- Events staff should welcome people on arrival and be in position at the exits to say 'thank you for coming – see you next time'.

- All walkie talkies should have earpieces so that the public cannot hear organisational messages. These could sometimes be misinterpreted and cause alarm.

- Events staff should never appear to be in a hurry, no matter how quickly they need to take action. This could cause unnecessary panic in the audience.

- If you ask people to be at the venue at a certain time, make sure that you (the organiser) are there punctually.

- Make sure you have a vet on site if animals are involved.

g) event ideas

50s, 60s, 70s concert
Agricultural show
Air show
Antiques roadshow
Barn dance
Beer festival
Big band bash
Café jazz night
Cajun music concert
Carnival
Carnival of Venice
Celebration of cycling
Charity markets
Children's cinema programme
Children's fancy dress parade
Chinese New Year
Christmas carol singalong
Christmas concert with Dickens
Classical spectacular with special effects
Classic vehicle displays/rallies
Community fairs
Competitions in art, drama, poetry, etc
Cookery masterclass
Country and western concert
Country fair
Craft fair
Design of the future competition
Dickensian craft fayre
Disability awareness day
Ethnic food and drink fest
Fairgrounds – shows and rides
Family fund day
Fashion show
Firework display
Flower festival
Folk festival
Football festival
Fun run
Gardeners question time
Gladiators
Golf competition
Guided themed walks
Gymnastics display
Illuminations/light sculptures
Inter-denominational religious service
It's a Knockout
Jazz and blues festival

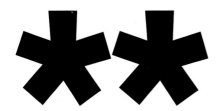 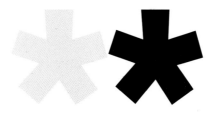

Kite flying
Laser display
Masked ball
Mediaeval jousting/mock battles
Messiah performance
Military band concert
Military tattoo
Motorcycle display
Music from around the world
Open air Shakespeare
Opera gala evening
Picnic in the park
Quad bikes competition
Real ale/beer festival
Rock concert
Roman chariot racing
Schools choral events
Soul night
Sponsored walks
Sports competitions
Steam rallies
Swing/40s-style show
Talent competition
Tea dance
Themed film festival
Themed market (French, Christmas, mediaeval)
Trade exhibition
Treasure hunt
Tribute bands night
Victorian evening in the town
Wild west spectacular
Youth orchestra concert

h) helpful organisations

The following is a list of important organisations who have something to offer in support of your event organisation efforts.

Arts Council for Northern Ireland (The)
181 Stranmillis Road
Belfast BT9 5DU
telephone: 01232 663591
fax: 01232 661715

Arts Council of England (The)
14 Great Peter Street
London SW1P 3NQ
telephone: 0171 333 0100
fax: 0171 973 6590

Association for Business Sponsorship of the Arts (The)
Nutmeg House
60 Gainsford Street
Butler's Wharf
London SE1 2NY
telephone: 0171 378 8143
fax: 0171 407 7527

Association of British Professional Conference Organisers
Dresden House
51 High Street
Evesham
Worcs WR11 4DA
telephone: 01386 422408
fax: 01386 422465

Association of Conference Executives
Riverside House
High Street
Huntingdon
Cambs PE18 6SG
telephone: 01480 457595
fax: 01480 412863

Association of Exhibition Organisers (The)
113 High Street
Benchamsted
Herts HP4 2DJ
telephone: 01442 873331
fax: 01442 875551

Association of Metropolitan Authorities (The)
35 Great Smith Street
Westminster
London SW1P 3BJ
telephone: 0171 222 8100
fax: 0171 222 0878

**Association of Playing Fields Officers and
Landscape Managers (The)**
See ISRM

Automobile Association
Lister Point
Sherrington Way
Basingstoke
Hampshire RG22 4DQ
telephone: 0345 697873
fax: 01256 491449

AVT Limited
AVT House
Stone Street
Brighton BN1 2HB
telephone: 01273 821344
fax: 01273 821451

Boldscan Limited
Tonedale Mills
Wellington
Somerset TA21 0AB
telephone: 01823 665849
fax: 01823 665850

British Association of Conference Destinations
1st Floor
Elizabeth House, Suffolk Street
Queensway
Birmingham B1 ILS
telephone: 0121 616 1400
fax: 0121 616 1364

British Council (The)
10 Spring Gardens
London SW1A 2BN
0171 389 4938
0171 389 4058

British Exhibition Contractors Association (The)
Kingsmere House
Graham Road
London SW19 3SR
0181 543 3888
0181 543 4036

British Exhibition Venues Association
C/O Alexandra Palace
Wood Green
London N22 4AY
0181 365 2121
0181 883 3999

British Federation of Music Festivals
Festivals House
198 Park Lane
Macclesfield
Cheshire SK11 6UD
01625 428297
01625 503229

British Hotels, Restaurants and Caterers Association
40 Duke Street
London W1M 6HR
0171 499 6641
0171 355 4596

British Institute of Professional Photography
2 Almwell End
Ware
Herts SG12 9HN
01920 464011
01920 487056

British Olympic Association
1 Church Row
Wandsworth Plain
London
SW18 1PH
0181 871 2677
0181 871 9104

Business in Sport and Leisure Limited
17A Chartfield Avenue
Putney
London SW15 6DX
0181 780 2377
0181 788 2277

Cadw - Welsh Historic Monuments
2 Fitzalan Road
Cardiff CF2 1UY
01222 500200
01222 500300

CCH Editions Limited
(Croner's *Reference Book for VAT*)
Telford Road
Bicester
Oxfordshire OX6 0XD
01869 253300
01869 874702

Central Council of Physical Recreation
Francis House
Francis Street
London SW1P 1DE
0171 828 3163
0171 630 8820

Charity Aid Foundation
48 Pembury Road
Tonbridge
Kent TN9 2JD
01732 520000
01732 520001

Charity Commission (The)
14 Ryder Place
London SW1Y 6AH
0171 210 4477
0171 210 4559

Civic Trust (The)
17 Carleton House Terrace
London SW1Y 5AW
0171 930 0914
0171 321 0180

Complete Talent Agency
The Entertainment Shop
1346 London Road
Leigh-on-Sea
Essex SS9 2UH
01702 478787
01702 478770

Convention of Scottish Local Authorities (COSLA)
Rosebery House
Haymarket Terrace
Edinburgh EH12 5XZ
0131 374 9200
0131 346 0055

Corporate Hospitality Association
PO Box 67
Kingswood
Hadworth
Surrey KT20 6LG
01737 833963
01737 833507

Countryside Commission (The)
John Dower House
Crescent Place
Cheltenham
Gloucestershire GL50 3RA
01242 531381
01242 584270

Countryside Council for Wales (The)
Ladywell House
Newtown
Powys SY16 1RD
01686 626799
01686 629556

Crafts Council
44A Pentonville Road
London N1 9BY
0171 278 7700
0171 837 6891

Design Council (The)
34 Bow Street
London WC2E 7DL
0171 420 5200
0171 420 5300

Design Council for Scotland (The)
72 St. Vincent's Street
Glasgow G2 5KN
0141 221 6121
0141 221 8799

English Heritage
The Historic Buildings and Monuments Commission
Fortress House
23 Saville Row
London W1X 2HE
0171 973 2000
0171 973 3001

English Regional Arts Boards
5 City Road
Winchester
Hampshire SO23 8SD
01962 851063
01962 842033

English Sports Council (The)
16 Upper Woburn Place
London WC1H 0QP
0171 273 1500
0171 383 5740

English Tourist Board/British Tourist Authority
Thames Tower
Black Road
London W6 9PL
0181 846 9000
0181 563 0302

Eve Barriers Ltd
30/34 Weir Road
Wimbledon
London SW19 8UG
0181 879 8807
0181 879 8808

Event Services Association (The)
8 Home Farm
Ardington
Oxfordshire OX12 8PN
01235 821820
01235 862200

Exhibition Industry Federation
PO Box 980
London SW11 5JB
0171 582 6899
0171 793 0293

Forestry Commission
231 Corstorphine Road
Edinburgh EH12 7AT
0131 334 0303
0131 316 4344

Mike Fulford
Leisure Advice
18 Curlew Hill
Morpeth
Northumberland NE61 3SH
telephone: 01670 516843

Health Start
1st Floor
Gateway House
Piccadilly South
Manchester M60 7LP
0161 237 2064
0161 237 2723

Hire Association of Europe
722 College Road
Erdington
Birmingham B44 0AJ
0121 377 7707
0121 382 1743

Historic Scotland
20 Brandon Street
Edinburgh EH3 5RA
0131 668 8600
0131 668 8789

Hotel and Catering Training Board
International House
High Street
Ealing
London W5 5DB
0181 579 2400
0181 840 6217

Hotel, Catering and Institutional Management Association
191 Trinity Road
London SW17 7HN
0181 672 4251
0181 682 1707

ILAM Services Limited
ILAM House
Lower Basildon
Reading
Berkshire RG8 9NE
01491 874800
01491 874801

Institute of Leisure and Amenity Management (ILAM)
ILAM House
Lower Basildon
Reading
Berkshire RG8 9NE
01491 874800
01491 874801

Institute of Management (The)
3rd Floor
2 Savoy Court
The Strand
London WC2R 0EZ
0171 497 0580
0171 497 0463

Institute of Management Consultants
5th Floor
32/33 Hatton Garden
London EC1N 8DL
0171 584 7285
0171 831 4597

Institute of Marketing (The)
Moore Hall
Cookham
Maidenhead
Berks SL6 9QH
01628 427500
01628 427499

Institute of Public Relations
Gatehouse
St. John's Square
London EC1M 4DH
0171 253 5151
0171 490 0588

Institute of Sales and Marketing Management
Romeland House
Romeland Hill
St. Albans
Herts AL3 4ET
01727 812500
01727 833020

Institute of Sport and Recreation Management (ISRM)
Gifford House
36/38 Sherrard Street
Melton Mowbray
Leics LE13 1XJ
01664 565531
01664 501155

Institute of Sports Sponsorship (The)
Francis House
Francis Street
London SW1P 1DE
0171 828 8771
0171 630 8820

Institute of Travel and Tourism
113 Victoria Street
St Albans
Herts
AL1 3TJ
01727 854395
01727 847415

Insurex Expo-Sure Limited
The Pantiles House
2 Nevill Street
Royal Tunbridge Wells
Kent TN2 5TT
01892 511500
01892 510016

International Association for Professional Conference Organisers
40 Rue Washington
1050 Brussels
Belgium
332 6401808

International Special Events Society
7080 Hollywood Boulevard
Suite 410
Los Angeles
CA 90028, USA

Kalamazoo Security Print Limited
Security Print Division
Northfield
Birmingham B31 2NY
0121 256 2000
0121 256 2244

Law Society (The)
Law Society's Hall
113 Chancery Lane
London WC2A 1PL
0171 242 1222
0171 405 9522

Library Association (The)
7 Ridgmount Street
London WC1 7AE
0171 636 7543
0171 436 7218

Local Government Association
26 Chapter Street
London SW1P 4ND
0171 664 3053
0171 664 3008

Local Government Management Board
Layden House
76-86 Turnmill Street
London EC1M 5QU
0171 296 6600
0171 296 6666

Market Research Society (The)
15 Northburgh Street
London EC1V 0AH
0171 490 499
0171 490 0608

Mellor, Penny
Basement Flat
8 Southern Street
London N1 9AY
0171 837 2239

Mobile and Outside Caterers Association of Great Britain (The)
Centre Court
1301 Stratford Road
Hall Green
Birmingham B28 9HH
0121 693 7000
0121 693 7100

Museums Association (The)
42 Clerkenwell Close
London EC1R 0PA
0171 250 1836
0171 2501929

Made-Up Textiles Assocation (The)
42 Heath Street
Tamworth
Staffordshire B79 7JH
01827 52337
01827 310827

National Association for Local Councils
109 Great Russell Street
London WC1B 3LD
0171 637 1865
0171 436 7451

National Association of Exhibition Hall Owners
The National Exhibition Centre
Birmingham B40 1NT
0121 780 4141
0121 782 2655

National Exhibitors Association
29 Market Square
Biggleswade
Bedfordshire SG18 8AQ
01767 316255
01767 316430

National Federation of Community Organisations
8/9 Upper Street
Islington
London N1 0PQ
0171 226 0184
0171 354 9670

National Federation of Music Societies
Francis House
Francis Street
London SW1P 1DA
0171 828 7320
0171 828 5504

National Outdoor Events Association (The)
7 Hamilton Way
Wallington
Surrey SM6 9NJ
0181 669 8121
0181 647 1128

National Playing Fields Association (The)
25 Ovington Square
London SW3 1LQ
0171 584 6445
0171 5881 2402

National Trust (The)
36 Queen Anne's Gate
London SW1H 9AS
0171 222 9251
0171 222 5097

National Trust for Scotland (The)
5 Charlotte Square
Edinburgh EH2 4DU
0131 226 5922
0131 243 9501

Northern Ireland Tourist Board
River House
48 High Street
Belfast BT1 2DS
01232 231221
01232 310933

Pains Fireworks
Whiteparish
Salisbury
Wiltshire SP5 2SD
01794 884040
01794 884015

Performing Arts Management Limited
Canal 7
Clarence Mill
Bollington, Macclesfield
Cheshire SK10 5JZ
01625 575681
01625 572839

Performing Rights Society Limited
29/33 Berner Street
London W1P 4AA
0171 580 5544
0171 631 4138

Production Services Association
Hawks House
School Passage
Kingston Upon Thames
Surrey KT1 3DU
0181 392 0180
0181 392 0181

Regan Cowland Associates
Television Centre
Vinters Park
Maidstone
Kent ME14 5NZ
01622 684507/8
01622 684660

Royal Fine Art Commission (The)
7 St James' Square
London SW1Y 4JU
0171 839 6537
0171 839 8475

Scottish Arts Council (The)
19 Charlotte Square
Edinburgh EH2 4DF
0131 226 6051
0131 225 9833

Scottish Civic Trust (The)
24 George Square
Glasgow G2 1EF
0141 221 1466
0141 248 6952

Scottish Convention Bureau
Business Travel Department
Scottish Tourist Board
23 Ravelston Terrace
Edinburgh EH4 3EW
0131 332 2433
0131 343 1844

Scottish Sports Council (The)
Caledonia House
South Gyle
Edinburgh EH12 9DQ
0131 317 7200

Scottish Tourist Board (The)
23 Ravelston Terrace
Edinburgh EH4 3EU
0131 332 2433
0131 313 1513

Sponsorship Association (The)
Dalby House
396-398 City Road
London EC1V 2QA
0171 713 7000
0171 713 2999

Sports Council for Wales (The)
Sophia Gardens
Cardiff CF1 9SW
01222 300547
01222 300600

SPRITO
24 Stephenson Way
London NW1 2HD
0171 388 7755
0171 388 9733

Stagesafe/South Western Management
13 Portland Road
Street
Somerset BA16 9PX
01458 445186
01458 841186

Tourism Society
26 Chapter Street
London SW1P 4ND
0171 834 0461
0171 932 0238

Two Four Productions Limited
Quay West Studios
Old Newnham
Plymouth PL7 5BH
01752 345424
01752 344224

UK Athletics
30A Harborne Road
Edgbaston
Birmingham B15 3AA
0121 456 5098
0121 456 4998

UK Sports Council (The)
Walkenden House
10 Melton Street
London NW1 2EB
0171 380 8000
0171 380 8025

Wales Tourist Board (The)
8/14 Bridge Street
Cardiff CF1 2EE
01222 499909
01222 485031

Welsh Arts Council (The)
9 Museum Place
Cardiff CF1 2NX
01222 376500
01222 221447

West Berkshire Council
Market Place
Newbury
Berks RG14 5LD
01635 424000
01635 519431

Zap Productions Ltd
7A Middle Street
Brighton
East Sussex BN1 1AL
01273 821588
01273 206960

Don't forget to make use of telephone directories, *Yellow Pages* and local directories (often handed out by the press and other media, they can prove to be invaluable). Most importantly your local library is a goldmine of valuable information.

i) reading list

Books

It is difficult to obtain specifically relevant publications but the following are relevant and useful:

American Sport Education Program (1996) *Event Management for Sport Directors*, Human Kinetics Publishers, Inc

Badmin, P., Coombs, M. and Rayner, G. (1988) *Leisure Operational Management - Volume 1: Facilities*, Longman/ILAM Leisure Management Services

Barbour, S. - Editor, *Arts Festivals in Britain and Ireland*, Rhinegold Publishing Limited

Batterham, G. - Editor (1992) *A Practical Approach to the Administration of Leisure and Recreation Services - 4th Edition*, Croner Publications Limited, Kingston-upon-Thames

Brown, M. (1992) *Successful Project Management in a Week*, Hodder and Stoughton

Briner, W., Geddes, M. and Hastings, C. (1990) *Project Leadership*, Gower Publishing Company

Brown, P. and Hackett, F. (1990) *Managing Meetings*, Collins

Business Entertainment (1994), Langston Scott Limited

Buttrick, R. (1997) *The Project Workout*, Pitman Publishing

Byl, J. (1990) *Organizing Successful Tournaments*, Leisure Press

Chestnutt, K. (1993) *Corporate Event Services*, Showcase Publications

Coltman, M.M. (1989) *Tourism Marketing*, Van Nostrand Reinhold

Daily Telegraph (1986) *How to Set Up and Run Conferences and Meetings*, Telegraph Publications

Druce, R. and Carter, S. (1988) *The Marketing Handbook - A Guide for Voluntary and Non-Profit Making Organisations*, National Extension College

English Tourist Board, *The Give and Take of Sponsorship*

English Tourist Board, *How to Organise an Event*

English Tourist Board, *Putting on the Style*

Festival Welfare Services (1990) *Co-ordinating Welfare Services at Festivals*, Festival Welfare Services

Fleming, I (1994) *Training Needs Analysis for the Leisure Industry*, Longman Group Limited

French, Y (1994) *Public Relations for Leisure and Tourism*, Longman

Goldblatt, J.J. (1997) *Special Events: The Art and Science of Celebration*, Von Nostrand Reinhold

Goldblatt, J (1997) *Special Events: Best Practice in Modern Event Management*

Hall, C.M. (1992) Hallmark Tourist Events - *Impacts, Management and Planning*, Bellhaven Press, London

Haynes, M.E. (1989) *Project Management - From Idea to Implementation*, Kogan Page Limited

Health and Safety Commission (1991) *A Guide to Health, Safety and Welfare at Pop Concerts and Other Similar Events*, Home Office

Health & Safety Executive (1988) *Essentials of Health & Safety at Work*, HMSO

Health & Safety Executive (1996) *Managing Crowds Safely*, HMSO

Home Office and Scottish Office (1990) *Guide to Safety at Sports Grounds*, HMSO

Institute of Leisure and Amenity Management (1997) *Consult the Professionals*, ILAM Services Consultancy Practice

Jeferson, A. and Lickorish, L., (1991) *Marketing Tourism*, 2nd Edition, Longman UK

Lance, S. and Lance, J., *The Showman's Directory*, Brook House, Surrey

Lawrie, A. (1996) *The Complete Guide to Creating and Managing New Projects for Charities and Voluntary Organisations*, Directory of Social Change

Leslie, D. - Editor (1995) *Tourism and Leisure - Perspectives on Provision*, LSA Publications

Lock, D. (1992) *Project Management - 5th Edition*, Gower Publishing Company Limited

Melnike, C.J. and Wilkinson, D.G. (1992) *Community Services Marketing*, Wilkinson Information Group Inc and Marketing Minds International

National Outdoor Events Association (1993) *Code of Practice for Outdoor Events Other than Pop Concerts and Raves*

Passingham, S. (1993) *Organising Local Events*, Directory of Social Change

Passingham, S. (1995) *Good Ideas for Raising Serious Money*, Directory of Social Change

Richards, B. (1992) *How to Market Tourist Attractions, Festivals and Special Events: A Practical Guide to Maximising Visitor Attendance and Income*, Longman

Rolfe, H. (1992) *Arts Festivals in the UK*, Policy Studies Institute

Rutherford, D. (1990) *Introduction to the Conventions, Expositions and Meetings Industry*, Van Nostrand Reinhold

Sayers, P. (1991) *Managing Sport and Leisure Facilities - A Guide to Competitive Tendering*, E & F N Spon

Scott, M. (1988) *Law and Leisure Services Management*, Longman UK

Scott, M. (1985) *The Law of Public Leisure Services*, Sweet and Maxwell

Scottish Sports Council (1980) *Major Events - An Organisation Manual*

Seekings, D., *How to Organise Effective Conferences and Meetings*, Kogan Page Limited

Stier, Jr. W. F. (1994) *Fund raising for Sport and Recreation - Step by Step Plans for 70 Successful Events*, Human Kinetics Publishers

Tancred, B. and Tancred, G. (1992) *Leisure Management*, Hodder & Stoughton

Taylor, Outhart et al (1996) *Developing Customer Service in Leisure and Tourism for Advanced GNVQ*, Harper Collins Publishers Limited

Torkildsen, G. (1991) *Leisure and Recreation Management - 2nd Edition*, E & F N Spon

Townley, S. and Grayson, E., *Sponsorship of Sports, Arts and Leisure - Law, Tax and Business Relationships*, Sweet and Maxwell

Ward, D. (1993) *Assignments in Leisure and Tourism for GNVQ: Book 2*, Stanley Thornes

Watt, D. C. (1992) *Leisure and Tourism Events Management and Organisation Manual*, Longman Group UK Limited

Watt, D. C. (1998) *Event Management in Leisure and Tourism*, Addison Wesley Longman

Watt, D. C. (1998) *Sports Management and Administration*, E & F N Spon

Welch, D. (1995) *Managing Public Use of Parks*, Open Spaces and Countryside, Pitman Publishing 1995

Wilkinson, D. (1988) *The Event Management and Marketing Institute 1*, IBD

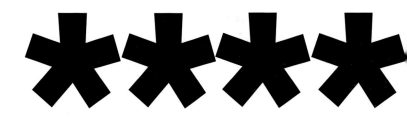

Journals

The CCL Guide, Conference Care Limited

Code of Practice for Outdoor Events - Other Than Pop Concerts and Raves - 1st Edition (January 1993) National Outdoor Events Association

The Conference Blue Book and The Conference Green Book, Spectrum Publishing

The Exhibition Data Book, Reid Information Services Limited

Hobsons Sponsorship Data Book (Annually) Hobson's Publishing Limited

Journal of Sport Management - Volume 11 - Number 3 (July 1997) Human Kinetics Publishers, Inc

Journal of Sport Management - Volume 10 - Number 3 (July 1997) Human Kinetics Publishers, Inc

Leisure Services Year Book (Annually) Longman UK Limited

Marketing Leisure Services, Leisure Features

Outdoor Events Guide, (Annually) Outdoor Events Publications Limited

Shades of Green - Working Towards Green Tourism in the Countryside (Conference Proceedings - 1990) Fielder Green Associates

Voluntary but not Amateur - A Guide to the Law for Voluntary Organisations and Community Groups - 4th Edition (October 1994) London Voluntary Service Council

Various publications of the Arts Councils and Sports Councils of England, Scotland, Wales and Northern Ireland and the Health and Safety Executive

j) press list (see BRAD for more extensive listings)

trade journals

magazine: **Access All Areas** (events)
publisher: Inside Communications Ltd
    Bank House
    23 Warwick Road
    Coventry CV1 2EW
tel: 01203 230333
fax: 01203 252241

magazine: **All Sport and Leisure Monthly** (sport)
publisher: All Sport and Leisure
    Graphic House
    3 High Road
    Ickenham
    Middlesex UB10 8LE
tel: 01895 679333
fax: 01895 677830

magazine: **Arts Business Magazine** (arts)
publisher: Arts Intelligence Ltd
    PO Box 358
    Cambridge CB4 3FP

magazine: **Conference and Exhibition Fact Finder**
    (events)
publisher: Batiste Publications Ltd
    Pembroke House
    Campsbourne Road
    Hornsey
    London N8 7PE
tel: 0181 340 3291
fax: 0181 341 4840

magazine: **Encore** (arts)
publisher: 240 Tolworth Rise South
    Surbiton
    Surrey KT5 9NB

magazine: **Environmental Health News** (environment)
publisher: Chadwick House Group Ltd
    Chadwick Court
    15 Hatfields
    London SE1 8DJ
tel: 0171 827 9928
fax: 0171 827 5883

magazine: **Healthlines** (health)
publisher: Health Education Authority
Trevelyan House
30 Great Peter Street
London SW1P 2HW
tel: 0171 222 5300
fax: 0171 413 8900

magazine: **Journal of Further and Higher Education**
(education)
publisher: National Association of Teachers in F&HE
27 Britannia Street
London WC1X 9JP
tel: 0171 837 3636
fax: 0171 837 4403

magazine: **Leisure and Countryside Programmes**
(leisure)
publisher: BBC
Pebble Mill Road
Birmingham B5 7QQ
tel: 021 414 8888
fax: 0121 414 8634

magazine: **Leisure Business** (leisure)
publisher: Wharncliffe Publishing Ltd
47 Church Street
Barnsley
South Yorkshire S70 2AS

magazine: **Leisure Management** (leisure)
publisher: The Leisure Media Company Ltd
Portmill House
Portmill Lane
Hitchin
Herts SG5 1DJ
tel: 01462 431385
fax: 01462 433909

magazine: **Leisure Week** (leisure)
publisher: Centaur Communications Limited
St Giles House
50 Poland Street
London W1V 4AX
tel: 0171 439 4222
fax: 0171 439 8065

magazine: **Local Authority News** (local government)
publisher: Nestron Ltd
68 Middle Abbey Street
Dublin 1
Republic of Ireland

magazine: **Local Council Review** (local government)
publisher: Plus PR Ltd
Press House
130A Godington Road
Ashford
Kent TN23 1LJ
tel: 01233 643574
fax: 01233 641816

magazine: **Local Government Chronicle**
(local government)
publisher: EMAP Business Communications
33-39 Bowling Green Lane
London EC1R 0DA
tel: 0171 505 8400
fax: 0171 278 9509

magazine: **Local Government Executive**
(local government)
publisher: Tempus House of Publishers
3rd Floor
Fourways House
57 Hilton Street
Manchester M1 2EJ
tel: 0161 237 1007
fax: 0161 237 1006

magazine: **Local Government News** (local government)
publisher: B & M Publications (London) Ltd
PO Box 13
Hereford House
Bridle Path
Croydon
Surrey CR9 4NL
tel: 0181 680 4200
fax: 0181 681 5049

magazine: **Marketing Event** (events)
publisher: Haymarket Business Publications Ltd
174 Hammersmith Road
London W6 7JP
tel: 0171 413 4366
fax: 0171 413 4514

magazine: **Mirror** (education)
publisher: 1 Canada Square
Canary Wharf
London E14 5DT

magazine: **Municipal Journal** (local government)
publisher: 32 Vauxhall Bridge Road
London SW1V 2SS
tel: 0171 973 6401
fax: 0171 233 5052

magazine: **Recreation** (sport)
publisher: ISRM
Giffard House
36-38 Sherrard Street
Melton Mowbray LE13 1XJ
tel: 01664 65531
fax: 01664 501155

magazine: **Scottish Local Government Information Unit**
(local government)
publisher: Scottish Local Government Information Unit
Room 507/511
Baltic Chambers
50 Wellington Street
Glasgow G2 6HJ

magazine: **Sports Industry** (sport)
publisher: 11 Abbey Business Centre
Ingate Place
London SW8 3NS
tel: 0171 498 0177
fax: 0171 498 9545
sport

magazine: **Sports News** (sport)
publisher: Sports Council for Wales
Sophia Gardens
Cardiff CF1 9SW

magazine: **The Leisure Manager** (leisure)
publisher: Institute of Leisure and Amenity Management
ILAM House
Lower Basildon
Reading
Berkshire RG8 9NE
tel: 01491 874800
fax: 01491 874801

magazine: **The Insider** (arts)
publisher: Arts Council
14 Great Peter Street
London SW1 3NQ

magazine: **Total Sport** (sport)
publisher: EMAP Metro Ltd
5th Floor, Mappin House
4 Winsley Street
London W1N 7AR
tel: 0171 436 1515
fax: 0171 323 0276

national newspapers

magazine: **The Daily Telegraph** (leisure)
publisher: The Telegraph Group Ltd
1 Canada Square
Canary Wharf
London E14 5DT
tel: 0171 538 5000
fax: 0171 538 6242

magazine: **The Guardian** (leisure)
publisher: Guardian Newspapers Ltd
119 Farringdon Road
London EC1R 3ER
tel: 0171 278 2332
fax: 0171 278 1449

magazine: **The Independent** (leisure)
publisher: Newspaper Publishing plc
1 Canada Square
Canary Wharf
London E14 3AP
tel: 0171 293 2000

magazine: **The Independent on Sunday** (leisure)
publisher: Newspaper Publishing plc
1 Canada Square
Canary Wharf
London E14 3AP
tel: 0171 293 2000

magazine: **The Observer** (leisure)
publisher: Guardian Newspapers Ltd
119 Farringdon Road
London EC1R 3ER
tel: 0171 278 2332
fax: 0171 278 1449

magazine: **The Stage** (arts)
publisher: Stage Newspapers Limited
47 Bermondsey Street
London SE1 3XT
tel: 0171 403 1818
fax: 0171 378 0480

magazine: **The Sunday Telegraph** (leisure)
publisher: The Telegraph Group Ltd
1 Canada Square
Canary Wharf
London E14 5DT
tel: 0171 538 5000
fax: 0171 538 6242

magazine: **The Sunday Times** (leisure)
publisher: Times Newspapers Ltd
P O Box 484
Virginia Street
London E1 9BL
tel: 0171 782 5000
fax: 0171 481 9313

magazine: **The Times** (leisure)
publisher: Times Newspapers Ltd
P O Box 496
Virginia Street
London E1 9XT
tel: 0171 782 5000
fax: 0171 481 9313

magazine: **Times Higher Education Supplement**
(education)
publisher: Times Newspapers Ltd
Admiral House
66-68 East Smithfield
London E1 9XY
tel: 0171 782 3000
fax: 0171 782 3333

evaluation

If you have read through all of this text, you are probably
now evaluating it but we do hope that you have also
evaluated its constituent parts on an ongoing basis.

So it should be with your event!

Events need a full evaluation, both at the end and during
implementation. This is not just an end debriefing session
but also a monitoring system to be used throughout.

Everyone involved in delivering the event should be
included in the evaluation process. They all have something
to contribute, they have all acquired experience that can
contribute to continually improving good practice. All staff,
paid and voluntary, should be consulted.

Evaluation should be:
- ongoing
- comprehensive
- consultative
- involving all customers
- continuous
- recorded for future reference
- compared to event objectives
- built on for future action

conclusion

The authors are aware that not every aspect of event management is covered in this book. The subject is very diverse, with most events being a one-off experience, but we have tried to cover the fundamental principles of event management.

Having drawn upon the wisdom of this text, you should now be better placed to organise your events. That said, you will not know everything – nobody ever does!

You will still need to plan carefully and if you do not know something - ask someone - perhaps one of the contributors to this book. Do not make your own mistakes, that is not the best way to learn. This text is best used to dip into on an 'as and when' basis, to help you remember, to inform, to refresh your memory about various aspects of event organisation. We can all do it better with the advice and support of others.

Event organisation is great fun, and very rewarding, if done properly; that comes through knowledge, hard work and experience.

The fundamental message is:

- know what and why you are doing it
- plan
- pay attention to detail
- deliver for your customers
- evaluate your performance

The authors wish you well in your event organising career.